T0329430

THE MASAI LANGUAGE

THE MASAI LANGUAGE

GRAMMATICAL NOTES

TOGETHER WITH A

VOCABULARY

COMPILED BY

HILDEGARDE HINDE

CAMBRIDGE:

AT THE UNIVERSITY PRESS.

1901

CAMBRIDGE
UNIVERSITY PRESS

University Printing House, Cambridge CB2 8BS, United Kingdom

Published in the United States of America by Cambridge University Press, New York

Cambridge University Press is part of the University of Cambridge.

It furthers the University's mission by disseminating knowledge in the pursuit of education, learning and research at the highest international levels of excellence.

www.cambridge.org
Information on this title: www.cambridge.org/9781107669901

First published 1901
First paperback edition 2014

A catalogue record for this publication is available from the British Library

ISBN 978-1-107-66990-1 Paperback

PREFACE.

THE following small work on the Masai language was compiled by me during two years spent among the Masai people. What I learnt was learnt directly from the Masai, and with no middleman in the way of Swahíli or other native interpreters. My excuse for undertaking a work of this description, without the special philological qualifications, is that I could converse freely with, and be fully understood by, any Masai; and that I could also well understand any Masai either talking to me or among themselves.

As my methods of learning and construing the language were not scientific but natural (if the contradistinction may be used), they may perhaps prove of some interest. During the first few weeks among the Masai I could not even hear sufficiently what they said to be able to write down anything intelligible, and my own attempts at saying a few words were equally unintelligible to them. Since I was familiar with Swahíli at the time it is improbable that this inability to hear or pronounce Masai should be ascribed to the fact that it is an African language. It is far more likely that the real difficulties of the language, intonation and accentuation, were hindering me, as Masai is undoubtedly difficult of pronunciation, construction and expression. When I was able to say a few words or sentences fairly correctly, I used them to every Masai I saw; and when they were said so that they were understood by a variety of people without hesitation I considered them correct. What one individual told me I told the next, and *vice versa*, thus correcting and recorrecting what I had originally written. The difficulties of forming rules—since it was, of course, impossible to convey any idea of grammar to the Masai themselves—I solved by making a large number of sentences all similarly constructed: if the Masai construction of these sentences proved similar (after having taken sufficient examples, say twenty or thirty) I concluded that I had the necessary evidence on which to base a rule. It will be readily understood that the deductions arrived at by these methods were adequate to supply the small number of grammatical rules contained in the following pages.

Two attempts only have previously been made at classifying Masai. The first is Ehrhardt's vocabulary (Würtemburg, 1857), which contains some 1000 words. To this no grammatical rules are appended; and since Krapf states in the preface to the vocabulary that Ehrhardt learnt all he knew of Masai from Swahílis at the coast, it is natural he should have fallen into the error of treating and writing Masai as a Bantu language, *i.e.* a language of prefixes. Sir H. H. Johnston's vocabulary and notes on the Masai language, contained in the *Kilima Njaro Expedition*, are more ambitious than Ehrhardt's small volume, though he has evidently based his theories of the formation of the language on Ehrhardt's work. That Sir H. H. Johnston had also no opportunity of conversing directly with wild Masai he himself testifies. The few Masai warriors whom he encountered at Mandara's court, and while he was actually travelling, he could only speak with through an interpreter, and the Wa-kwavi—from whom he learnt what he knew of the language—are not recognized by the wild Masai as members of their community. Sir H. H. Johnston states that the Wa-kwavi (their very name has been made Bantu) have intermarried with Bantus of all sorts; and it therefore

follows that their language will probably have adopted
many words other than Masai, and that the construction
is likely to have been altered to that of the peoples among
whom they live. I must take exception to the writing
of Masai as employed both by Ehrhardt and Sir H. H.
Johnston. Though it is quite possible that originally the
first syllables of Masai words denoted the gender, it is
now equally impossible to write or treat of these words as
separable from the first syllable. By so doing the language
is converted into a language of prefixes, and a wrong in-
terpretation is put on the words, since they are senseless
and unintelligible if used without the first syllables. As
inanimate objects are all neuter, and all animals (with the
exception of cow, sheep, goat and donkey—the domestic
animals of the Masai) are both masculine and feminine, the
theory that *ol* is representative of the masculine gender and
n or *en* of the feminine, can hardly hold good: for example,
orldia is equally dog or bitch, *orrgenoss* is equally a male or
female crocodile, *mparnass* is equally a male or female
duyker, *nottorrangi* is either a male or a female chameleon.
What further bears out the theory that the current signifi-
cation, of these first syllables, at any rate, is *not* denominative
of gender, is the fact that "father" in Masai is *baba*, and
"mother" *yeyu*, neither of these important words commencing with the gender prefix.

It seems, for various reasons, improbable that the Masai
first syllables can be regarded by the Masai themselves as
indicative of gender. Their distinction between male and
female is very marked, the female being regarded as quite
inferior; and bearing out this hypothesis Sir H. H. Johnston
says:—" masculine *ol* may be taken as meaning strong, big,
masculine...... The article *en* is mainly feminine in its
significance, but it also gives a diminutive, depreciatory,
weakened, playful, or affectionate character to the word it

precedes" (the *Kilima Njaro Expedition*, pages 455, 456).
It is unlikely that such important words as $\left.\begin{array}{l}\text{God}\\\text{rain}\end{array}\right\} = ngai,$
fire = *ngima*, food = *nda*, country = *ngop*, day or sun = *ngolong*,
forest = *endim*, gun = *endiul*, meat = *engeringu*, game = *ngwess*,
grass = *engojeta*, etc., etc. should denote the feminine gender.
But according to Sir H. H. Johnston's theory this follows
unless they can be considered as representative of the
characteristics enumerated. The examples indicated should
sufficiently prove that the Masai significance of these first
syllables is not that suggested by Sir H. H. Johnston.

I therefore consider the spelling of words as follows:
foot = ngaju, *en* (instead of *en*geju); donkey = sigiria, *os*;
elephant = dome, *ol*; arm = gaina, *en*;—is wrong, and in no
way descriptive of the language, or indicated by it.

Since the first syllable of Masai words must therefore be
regarded as almost invariably unchangeable, and as forming
part of the word itself, it seems inaccurate even to call it a
prefix. In Bantu languages one word is capable of having
a variety of prefixes attached to it, as for example: good =
-zuri, *m*zuri, *ma*zuri, *wa*zuri, *vi*zuri, *ki*zuri. Here, in the
first instance, the root of the word is given with a dash
preceding it, since it is impossible to indicate the necessary
prefix unless the noun qualified is known. But the writing
of Masai words in this manner is alien to the structure of
the language. For example the word "good" (*sidai*) in
Masai is used for nouns of all denominations:

> sidai orlaiyon = a good boy,
> sidai engitok = a good woman,
> sidai ngishu   = good cattle,
> sidai ngaji   = a good house,
> sidai nda   = good food,
> sidai orldia   = a good dog.

The verbs should surely be written in the infinitive or

the imperative. The roots, as given by Sir H. H. Johnston, convey little idea of the words intended to be represented by them, and can never be used conversationally in these forms. I must also disagree with his placing the personal pronoun before the verbs when they are conjugated. I have carefully conjugated and studied over 70 verbs, and in one case only—the verb "to bring"—do the personal pronouns precede the verb all through. In a great many verbs the abbreviations of "I" and "thou"—*a* or *i*—are used preceding the verbs, but the rest of the verb is usually conjugated with the pronouns following the verb. Most frequently only the first person singular takes the abbreviation and precedes the verb.

Since Joseph Thompson made us acquainted with the Masai the word has invariably been pronounced with a hissing *s*. This is incorrect: the accent is very markedly on the first syllable—Māsai—and the *s* is not sharp.

The difficulty of giving the right value to words in an unknown language has compelled me to adopt the long and the short accents. I have, however, done so as sparingly as possible, and only with regard to those words where the emphasis is so great that they would be unintelligible to the Masai if unaccented.

HILDEGARDE HINDE.

British East Africa, 1900.

EDITOR'S NOTE.

Owing to Mrs Hinde's absence in Africa it was necessary to leave the revision of her proofs in other hands. Any inaccuracies occurring in the text must, therefore, be ascribed to this fact.

E. C. M.

GRAMMATICAL RULES.

THERE are sounds in Masai corresponding to the following letters of the alphabet:

a b c d e g h i j k l m n o p r s t u w y

Besides these there are:

ä   ö   oi   ü   sh   ss   rr   ai

The vowels are pronounced as in Italian and the consonants as in English.

The spelling adopted is, as far as possible, phonetic, and the accents merely the short and long. It is impossible to represent many words in Masai without accents, or to give any adequate idea of the pronunciation, without occasionally using the aspirate: as :—*oshiagi* = also, *ishigo* = better, etc., in which words the aspirate is distinctly audible.

b and *p* are almost similar in pronunciation, and are practically interchangeable, as are also *g* and *k*.

The voice is frequently sunk at the end of the word, and should the word end with a consonant it is sometimes so slightly pronounced that it is difficult to distinguish it.

The *r*, which I have written as *rr*, is very pronounced, being sounded with a marked burr.

The *s* at the end of a word, and occasionally in the middle of a word, is sharply sounded as in hissing. This sound I have written as *ss*.

m and *n*, when commencing a word, and when followed by a consonant, are sounds of almost all African languages. The nearest approximation to their pronunciation is the slight sounding of the *m* in "mutter," and the *n* in "no":

they can neither be regarded as distinct syllables, nor must
they be sounded as apart from the rest of the word.

The accent in Masai usually falls on the first syllable in
words of two syllables, and in words of two or three syllables
most usually on the second, but occasionally on the third.
In words of more than three syllables the accent is usually
on the second syllable. The accentuation is, however, not
very regular, and in some words all the syllables are of equal
value.

Abbreviation of words, and the cutting off of final vowels
and even syllables is frequent and most confusing. In
speaking, the words are not distinctly pronounced, but
run on smoothly with no break, the syllables being often
swallowed and the voice so sunk at intervals that it is
difficult to catch all the words. The *liaison* is frequently
used. The Masai have a strong feeling for euphony, and
words are adapted and altered apparently for no other
reason. Where two words, one ending and the other beginning with a vowel, follow one another, consonants (gen-
erally *n*, *k*, or *b*) are sometimes introduced, as ainyo *b*erora =
why sleep?

(1)   The Personal Pronouns are:

		Singular		*Plural*
1st person	I	nanu	we	iog or eeog
2nd ,,	thou	iye	you	ndai or iye
3rd ,,	he, she, it	nenye or ninyi	they	nenje or ninji

(2)   Questions are formed in Masai merely by using an
interrogative tone of voice, as:

    I am ill   aemwi   Am I ill?   aemwi?

(3)   Negations are formed by prefixing the word "not,"
which is rendered by *meti* and its abbreviations *mer*, *me*
and *m*, or by the words *ete*, *etwa*, *etu*.

Meti is seldom used in full in conjunction with other words.

Mer is used, evidently for the sake of euphony, before words beginning with a consonant, except before those beginning with an *s*: for these *me* is used. *m* is used for words beginning with a vowel.

Not bad	mer torono	Not milk	mer gule
Not good	me sidai	Not large	me sabuk
I do not want	maiu	I do not know	maiulu
I am not going	etwaolo	He will not bring	eteaw
	I am not tired	eteanawri	

(4) There are no conjunctions in Masai. "And" is simply omitted, as:

The dog and cat	orldia embarrie (literally dog, cat)
The man and woman	eltungana engitok (man, woman)

O or *oi* are occasionally inserted between words supposed to connected with a conjunction, but this is probably for the sake of euphony, as in most instances the final vowel of the first word is dropped, as: you and I = *nan oiye*, instead of *nanu iye*; he and you = *neny oiye*, instead of *nenye iye*. It must be admitted that in both these instances the altered form is the more euphonious.

For the prepositions "with" and "for" there appear to be no words at all.

The preposition "in" (*atwa*) always precedes the noun it governs.

atwa ngaji	= in the house
atwa ngoshogi	= in the stomach
atwa engang	= in the kraal

(5) There are neither definite nor indefinite articles in Masai.

(6) There are three genders in Masai: masculine, feminine and neuter.

1—2

The same word is used for male and female animals, with
the exception of: sheep, goat, ass, cow, which have a
different word for the male and female.

All inanimate objects are neuter.

(7) Adjectives in Masai are invariable, and are only
altered for the sake of euphony: when, for example, an
adjective commencing with a vowel follows a substantive
ending with a vowel, it may, under these circumstances, take
a consonant preceding the vowel, as:

<table>
<tr><td>Red cloth</td><td>Hot water</td></tr>
<tr><td>engela kenyuki</td><td>ngare nairogua</td></tr>
</table>

(8) The place of the adjective is undefined: it may
either precede or follow the substantive, as:

<table>
<tr><td>A long house</td><td>A black goat</td></tr>
<tr><td>ērdo ngāiji</td><td>ndari nārok</td></tr>
</table>

(9) The numeral adjectives always follow the substantive, and usually end the sentence:

I see a hundred cows
Arradua ngishu īip.

(10) The numeral adjectives are as follows:

1 = nabu
2   ari or are
3   ūni
4   ungwun
5   miet
6   elle
7   nabishāna
8   issiet
9   nawdu or endōrroi
10   tomon
11   tomon obbo
12   tomon are
13   tomon ogūni

14 = tomon ungwun
15   tomon oimiet
16   tomon oiille
17   tomon nabishāna
18   tomon oissiet
19   tomon nawdo
20   tigitum
21   tigitum obbo
30   ossom
31   ossom obbo
40   arrtam
41   arrtam obbo
50   orrnom
51   orrnom obbo
60 = īp (which equals our 100. The Masai count in
       sixties, and a company of warriors is composed
       of 60 men)
Two sixties = īp ari
First = tangasaino
Last = korom.

Like all primitive peoples the Masai count on their
fingers. The closed fist represents 5, the two closed fists 10.
For higher numbers the fists are moved up and down until
the multiplication has been made. To represent 60, or any
higher figure, the fingers of one hand are snapped, but if the
number be very large the fingers of both hands are snapped
several times.

(11) Adjectives are capable of declension, and follow
the same rules as verbs. They do not alter according to
gender, but almost invariably for the sake of euphony:
occasionally they take the same plural as the noun they
qualify. In some instances the auxiliary verb is in no way
represented, the adjective only being used with the personal

pronouns. In other instances the auxiliary verb is used, the adjective in both instances being declined.

I am ill	aemwi
Thou art ill	emweiye
He she or it is ill	emwenenye
We are ill	kemwesiog
You are ill	emwewe ndai
They are ill	ana imwiwi

I am tired	aranawei
Thou art tired	atanauriiye
He she or it is tired	kerenaure nenye
We are tired	keternauriawdisiog
You are tired	anaura ndai
They are tired	keranaura ata nenje

I am well	arabiëro
Thou art well	eraiiyebiëro
He she or it is well	biero ossenenye
We are well	kera biot
You are well	erarandai biot
They are well	aibio nenje

(12) The possessive adjective always follows the noun. The various words for each adjective are used for the sake of euphony:

Our boma	engangang
Our cows	ngishuung
My father	baba lai
My hand	ngaiinai

my	lai, elai or ai	our	enāang, ung, oog
thine	enino	your	eninyi, nyn, linyi
his hers its	enenye, eno	their	āasho, ejanggarr, enje

(13) All verbs in Masai are conjugated, and with a certain degree of regularity. In some cases the abbreviations of "I" and "thou" (a or i) are used preceding the verb, but almost invariably the pronoun follows the verb, which commences

the sentence. All negatives and interrogatives, however, precede the verbs:

I know	I do not know	What are you doing?
aiulu	*maiulu*	*ainyo endobera?*

The infinitive mood always commences with an *n* : frequently this *n* is simply prefixed to the first person singular, though the larger number of infinitives merely bear some general resemblance to the verb. Where the infinitive singular is formed by prefixing an *n* to the first person singular, the second and third persons singular also usually take an *n* instead of using the first person, as :

to go	*nalo*	1st person
	nilo	2nd person
	nelo	3rd person
to come	*nalotu*	1st person
	nelotu	2nd and 3rd persons

The persons plural all use one word, though this is often distinct from the singular. In cases where the infinitive simply bears a general resemblance to the verb, all the persons singular use this word. In many verbs the singular and plural have slightly different infinitives, though both invariably have the *n* prefix, as :

	Singular	*Plural*
to cut	*na*dung	*negi*dung
to catch	*ne*bong	*negi*bong
to bathe	*na*isoja	*nega*soja

(14) The present and future tenses of verbs are alike. The past tense is formed by prefixing the word *edeba* (finished) to the verb, which thus becomes an auxiliary verb.

(15) The verbs "to be" and "to have" always precede the noun: all other verbs follow it. The past tenses of these two verbs, if existent, are not in general use. The usual

method of expressing their past tense is by using the present tense with an adverb denoting time, as:

I am yesterday　　　　　　　　I have a cow last night
I am in Naivasha last moon.

The present tense of " to be " is:

	Singular		Plural
I am	*aad, ara* or *a*	we are	*kera* or *era iog*
thou art	*eraiiye, eata* or *e*	you are	*erara* or *erarandai*
he she is it	*eerda eera* or *ata nenye*	they are	*ana* or *eranenje* or *weji*

The present tense of "to have" is exactly the same as the present tense of " to be ": there is no distinction between the two verbs.

(16) There is an imperative mood, both singular and plural, to all verbs. The imperative singular almost invariably commences with *t* and the plural with *en* : both usually resemble the verb. Examples:

		Imp. Sing.	Imp. Plural
I sing	arrany	tarranya	endarrain
I climb	atakedu	tagedo	endagedi
I break	agil nanu	tegella	endegi
I say	etejo nanu	toojo	endojo

(17) Nouns in Masai form their plurals by affixes, though occasionally the middle syllables of the word may also be altered.

(18) There are nine regular methods of forming the plural ; they are as follows:

		Sing.	Plural	
(1)	i or oi or ni	engela	engelani	= clothes
		ndap	ndapi	= hand
		orlōrro	orlōrroi	= goat (male)
(2)	a or ia	oldulet	olduleta	= bottle
		essurutie	essorudia	= earring
		essondai	essondä	= wall

		Sing.	Plural	
(3)	u, tu	ingobirr	ingobirru	= feather
		emurrt	emurrtu	= neck
		oldonyi	elōnitu	= skin
(4)	n, in	ossesi	essessin	= body
		ōrgenoss	ergenossin	= crocodile
		mbarrda	mbarrdan	= horse
(5)	k, ak, ok	ngorraion	ngorroiok	= woman
		emoworr	mowarrak	= horn
		orlāmonon	lamonok	= beggar
(6)	g	ngaina	ngaieg	= arm
		ndāridigi	ndāridig	= bird
(7)	r or rr	ngera	ngerr	= sheep
		emossori	emossorr	= egg
		endōlu	endōluer	= axe
(8)	o	olashi	olasho	= calf
		endōlit	endōlo	= marrow
(9)	t	ollogurrto	ollogurrt	= caterpillar
		engumoru	engumurrt	= hole
		engias	engiaset	= work

(19) Two words—mother and twig—form their plurals by prefixes:

yeyu	*noi*yeyu
loom	*e*loom

I have found no trace of nouns forming their plurals with the prefixes *ku* or *k*.

(20) A large number of nouns form their plurals quite irregularly; some alter the first syllable or middle syllables, but in many instances the whole word is changed:

	Sing.	Plural
tick	orromashere	ellemasher
dance	ingirigura	maigurana
hippopotamus	ollomagaw	errmagawl
breast	orrigena	ellgiē
mark	orrborrnoto	irrgonot
chair	oloirika	lorrigaishi
kudu	emālo	miggibi

(21)   Some nouns are alike both in singular and plural:

sun or suns	ngolong
beard or beards	orrümünyi
flea or fleas	loisusu
fire or fires	ngima
father or fathers	baba

(22)   When used in conjunction with verbs of negation nouns are capable of conjugation:

I have not anything	maadatoki
Thou hast not anything	mieraisietoki
He she or it has not anything	meerasenenye
We have not anything	mieraiog
You have not anything	mierarasendai
They have not anything	keera nenje

(23)   The interrogatives "why" and "what" (*ainyo*) when preceding a noun, pronoun, adjective or verb, insert *b*, *be*, or *ba* between the two words, as: why sleep? *ainyo berora?* The entire interrogative may be omitted, with the exception of the final *o*, and written *oberora*, or even further abbreviated to *oba*.

Why go?	ainyo *b*elo?
Why good?	ainyo *b*asidai?
Why drink?	ainyo *b*eiōk?

VERBS.

Present or Future Tense   *Imperative Mood*

Infinitive of **to go** $= \begin{cases} \textbf{nalo} \\ \textbf{nillo} \\ \textbf{nello} \\ \textbf{nigïbu} \end{cases}$ (singular) (plural)

I go or will go	alo nanu		
Thou goest or wilt go	illoiye	Go thou	shomo
He she or it goes or will go	kello nenye		
We go or will go	kibuuyook		
You go or will go	eshomo ndai	Go you	anshom or mããbe
They go or will go	kebo nenje		

Infinitive of **to see** $= \begin{cases} \textbf{nadol} \text{ (singular)} \\ \textbf{negidol} \text{ (plural)} \end{cases}$

I see or will see	arradua nanu		
Thou seest or wilt see	etaduai iye	See thou	etadua
He she or it sees or will see	etadua nenye		
We see or will see	kiraduiog		
You see or will see	ertadua ndai	See you	etaduã
They see or will see	anaetadua		

Infinitive of **to want** $= \begin{cases} \textbf{naiyu} \\ \textbf{niyu} \\ \textbf{neyu} \\ \textbf{negiaiu} \end{cases}$ (singular) (plural)

I want or shall want	aiyu nanu		
Thou wantest or shalt want	iyu iye	Want thou	toomono
He she or it wants or will want	keyu or eyu nenye		
We want or shall want	kiyu iog		
You want or will want	iyu ndai	Want ye	toomono
They want or shall want	keyu nenje		

Present or Future Tense   *Imperative Mood*

Infinitive of **to bring** = $\begin{cases} \textbf{naiau} \\ \textbf{niyau} \\ \textbf{neyau} \end{cases}$ (singular)

$\textbf{negiau}$ (plural)

I bring or will bring	aiau nanu	
Thou bringest or wilt bring	yau iye	Bring thou iau
He she or it brings or will bring	eyau nenye	
We bring or will bring	iognaiau	
You bring or will bring	ndainaiau	Bring ye eau
They bring or will bring	anaiau	

Infinitive of **to return** = $\begin{cases} \textbf{narrinyo} \text{ (singular)} \\ \textbf{nigurinyo} \text{ (plural)} \end{cases}$

I return or will return	arrinyo nanu	
Thou returnest or wilt return	torrinyo iye	Return thou torrinyoi
He she or it returns or will return	errorinyi	
We return or will return	kerrinyoi yok	
You return or will return	irrinyoiyo ndai	Return ye torrininyi
They return or will return	anairrinyu	

Infinitive of **to hear** = $\begin{cases} \textbf{naning} \text{ (singular)} \\ \textbf{negining} \text{ (plural)} \end{cases}$

I hear or will hear	atoringu	
Thou hearest or wilt hear	itoringu	Hear thou toringu
He she or it hears or will hear	kerroninonginye	
We hear or will hear	kerroninong ossiog	
You hear or will hear	etonginong ndai	Hear ye endonyin
They hear or will hear	kerroninonginje	

Infinitive of **to come** = $\begin{cases} \textbf{nalotu} \\ \textbf{nilotu} \\ \textbf{neloto} \end{cases}$ (singular)

$\textbf{negibon}$ (plural)

I come or will come	ālotu	
Thou comest or wilt come	elotu iye	Come thou woo
He she or it comes or will come	elotu nenye	
We come or will come	kiboniog	
You come or will come	iētu ndai	Come ye ōotu or ōō
They come or will come	kietuaninji	

Present or Future Tense   *Imperative Mood*

Infinitive of **to make** = {**naitobera** (singular)
{**negindoberr** (plural)

I make or will make	airoberr nanu		
Thou makest or wilt make	endoberiye	Make thou	endobera
He she or it makes or will make	ketoberr ninyi		
We make or will make	kindoberra yōōg		
You make or will make	endobera ndai	Make ye	kitobera
They make or will make	kitoberr ninji		

Infinitive of **to know** = {**naiulu** (singular)
{**negiolog** (plural)

I know or shall know	nanu naiulu		
Thou knowest or wilt know	iye naiulu	Know thou	aiulu
He she or it knows or will know	eulu nenye		
We know or shall know	kiolo iog		
You know or will know	eololo ndai	Know ye	aiuloito
They know or will know	eolonenje		

Infinitive of **to love** = {**nanyorr** (singular)
{**negenyorr** (plural)

I love or will love	anyorr nanu		
Thou lovest or wilt love	enyorr iye	Love thou	tonyorra
He she or it loves or will love	kenyorr nenye		
We love or will love	enyossiyog		
You love or will love	kenyorr ndai	Love ye	tonyorr
They love or will love	kenyorr ninji		

Infinitive of **to give** = {**nenjog** or **naisho** (singular)
{**neginjog** (plural)

I give or will give	aiisho nanu		
Thou givest or wilt give	injoğ iye	Give thou	enjōōğ
He she or it gives or will give	ejenjoğenenye		
We give or will give	kenjoğ iog		
You give or will give	enjoshoğ ndai	Give ye	enjōōğ ninji
They give or will give	kishoğ eninji		

Present or Future Tense   *Imperative Mood*

Infinitive of **to kill** = $\begin{cases} \textbf{naying} \text{ or } \textbf{neying} \text{ (singular)} \\ \textbf{negiying} \text{ (plural)} \end{cases}$

I kill or will kill	aiyin nanu		
Thou killest or wilt kill	iyen iye	Kill thou	teyunga
He she or it kills or will kill	keyeng nenye		
We kill or will kill	kiyeng siog		
You kill or will kill	keyeng ndai	Kill ye	endeyeng
They kill or will kill	keyeng ninji		

Infinitive of **to carry** = $\begin{cases} \textbf{nanab} \text{ or } \textbf{naier} \text{ (singular)} \\ \textbf{negeer} \text{ (plural)} \end{cases}$

I carry or will carry	aiya nanu		
Thou carriest or wilt carry	$\begin{cases} \text{tanaba iye} \\ \text{eyaiyan iye} \end{cases}$	Carry thou	$\begin{cases} \text{tanabo} \\ \text{yaua iye} \end{cases}$
He she or it carries or will carry	$\begin{cases} \text{kenaba nenye} \\ \text{ewadu nenye} \end{cases}$		
We carry or will carry	keyau iōg		
You carry or will carry	yai ndai	Carry ye	ewāretar
They carry or will carry	keai ninyi		

Infinitive of **to finish** = $\begin{cases} \textbf{naideba} \text{ (singular)} \\ \textbf{negendeb} \text{ (plural)} \end{cases}$

I finish or will finish	aideba		
Thou finishest or wilt finish	edebaiye	Finish thou	idebi
He she or it finishes or will finish	edeba nenye		
We finish or will finish	kendeba iyog		
You finish or will finish	endeba ndai	Finish ye	endeba
They finish or will finish	edeba ninji		

Infinitive of **to fold** = $\begin{cases} \textbf{nagil} \text{ or } \textbf{naien} \text{ (singular)} \\ \textbf{negerred} \text{ (plural)} \end{cases}$

I fold or will fold	agil		
Thou foldest or wilt fold	teredaiye	Fold thou	teena
He she or it folds or will fold	tereda nenye		
We fold or will fold	ketereda iyog		
You fold or will fold	eterera ndai	Fold ye	endēēn
They fold or will fold	eterrda ninji		

Present or Future Tense　　　　*Imperative Mood*

Infinitive of **to fly** = {**nebirr** or **nebirri** (singular)
　　　　　　　　　　　　　{**negibirr** (plural)

I fly or will fly	aibidu		
Thou fliest or wilt fly	ibidoiye	Fly thou	eeda
He she or it flies or will fly	kibido nenye		
We fly or will fly	kibido iyok		
You fly or will fly	embido ndai	Fly ye	eeda
They fly or will fly	ebido ninji		

Infinitive of **to laugh** = {**nakweni** (singular)
　　　　　　　　　　　　　　{**nigigweni** (plural)

I laugh or will laugh	atagwenia		
Thou laughest or wilt laugh	igwen iye	Laugh thou	tagwenia
He she or it laughs or will laugh	katagwenia ninyi		
We laugh or will laugh	ketagwenia siog		
You laugh or will laugh	etagwenia ndai	Laugh ye	tagwenia bōōgi
They laugh or will laugh	ketagwenia ninji		

Infinitive of **to cut** = {**nadung** (singular)
　　　　　　　　　　　　　{**negidung** (plural)

I cut or will cut	atudung		
Thou cuttest or wilt cut	itudungoiye	Cut thou	tudungu
He she or it cuts or will cut	ketudungu nenye		
We cut or will cut	ketudung iog		
You cut or will cut	ketudung ndai	Cut ye	endudung
They cut or will cut	ketudungo nenje		

Infinitive of **to call** = {**naibot** or **nēebot** (singular)
　　　　　　　　　　　　　{**neginbot** (plural)

I call or will call	aiboto		
Thou callest or wilt call	emboto iye	Call thou	emboto
He she or it calls or will call	keboto nenye		
We call or will call	kimboto iog		
You call or will call	kimboto ndai	Call ye	emboto
They call or will call	kimboto ninji		

Present or Future Tense   *Imperative Mood*

$$\text{Infinitive of } \textbf{to catch} = \begin{cases} \textbf{nebong} \text{ (singular)} \\ \textbf{negibong} \text{ (plural)} \end{cases}$$

I catch or will catch	aïibonğ		
Thou catchest or wilt catch	embongaiye	Catch thou	emboonga
He she or it catches or will catch	kebonga ninyi		
We catch or will catch	embongaiyog		
You catch or will catch	embonga ndai	Catch ye	emboonga
They catch or will catch	embonga ninji		

$$\text{Infinitive of } \textbf{to climb} = \begin{cases} \textbf{naged} \text{ (singular)} \\ \textbf{negiged} \text{ (plural)} \end{cases}$$

I climb or will climb	atakedu		
Thou climbest or wilt climb	iked iye	Climb thou	tagedo
He she or it climbs or will climb	karagedo nenye *		
We climb or will climb	karagedo siog		
You climb or will climb	karageda ndai	Climb ye	endagedi
They climb or will climb	kegede ninji		

$$\text{Infinitive of } \textbf{to buy} = \begin{cases} \textbf{nainyangu} \text{ or } \textbf{nenyong} \text{ (singular)} \\ \textbf{neginyawng} \text{ (plural)} \end{cases}$$

I buy or will buy	ainyawngo		
Thou buyest or wilt buy	inyang iye	Buy thou	inyangu
He she or it buys or will buy	kemer nenye		
We buy or will buy	inyangu iog		
You buy or will buy	inyangu ndai	Buy ye	enyangu
They buy or will buy	inyangu nenje		

$$\text{Infinitive of } \textbf{to cook} = \begin{cases} \textbf{naierishu} \text{ or } \textbf{neyerr} \text{ (singular)} \\ \textbf{negiyerr} \text{ (plural)} \end{cases}$$

I cook or will cook	aierishu		
Thou cookest or wilt cook	iryerishoiye	Cook thou	taiara
He she or it cooks or will cook	iryerisho nenye		
We cook or will cook	iryerishoiiog		
You cook or will cook	enaiyerisho	Cook ye	endaierishu
They cook or will cook	iryerisho ninji		

* In this instance karagedo can be spelt karakedo, the g and k being interchangeable.

Present or Future Tense *Imperative Mood*

Infinitive of **to cry** = {**naisherr** (singular)
{**negenjerr** (plural)

I cry or will cry	aishera		
Thou criest or wilt cry	injeraiye	Cry thou	injēēra
He she or it cries or will cry	eisher nenye		
We cry or will cry	kinjera siog		
You cry or will cry	enai injerr	Cry ye	ēnjera
They cry or will cry	eshera ninji		

Infinitive of **to clean** = {**naworr** or **neworr** (singular)
{**negiworr**} (plural)
{**noor** }

I clean or will clean	aisoj nanu		
Thou cleanest or wilt clean	issōjī ye	Clean thou	essoja
He she or it cleans or will clean	kessōj ninyi		
We clean or will clean	kessojaiiog		
You clean or will clean	ana kessoj	Clean ye	essoja
They clean or will clean	essoj ninji		

Infinitive of **to bathe** or **wash** = {**naisoja** (singular)
{**negasoja** (plural)

I bathe or will bathe	aisoja		
Thou bathest or wilt bathe	essojai ye	Bathe thou	essojaiu
He she or it bathes or will bathe	kessoja nenye		
We bathe or will bathe	kessoja siog		
You bathe or will bathe	anakessoja	Bathe ye	essojaira
They bathe or will bathe	essoja nenje		

Infinitive of **to wait** = {**naanya** (singular)
{**neginanya** (plural)

I wait or shall wait	aanyo		
Thou waitest or wilt wait	taanyoiye	Wait thou	ndaishu
He she or it waits or will wait	keainyo nenye		
We wait or will wait	tianyiyoog		
You wait or will wait	anagiaīno	Wait ye	endaendai
They wait or will wait	tianyo nenje		

Present or Future Tense   *Imperative Mood*

Infinitive of **to bite** = { **nawon** or **naawŏn** (singular) / **negiwon** (plural) }

I bite or will bite	atoonyo		
Thou bitest or wilt bite	atoon iye	Bite thou	toonyo
He she or it bites or will bite	kawenenye		
We bite or will bite	kaweniog		
You bite or will bite	anakawan	Bite ye	endoonyn
They bite or will bite	kawanenje		

Infinitive of **to sleep** = { **nairora** or **nerora** (singular) / **negirora** (plural) }

I sleep or will sleep	airora nanu		
Thou sleepest or wilt sleep	erora iye	Sleep thou	erorai
He she or it sleeps or will sleep	erora nenye		
We sleep or will sleep	erora iog		
You sleep or will sleep	erora ndai	Sleep ye	erraga
They sleep or will sleep	anagerora		

Infinitive of **to break** = { **nagil** or **negil** (singular) / **negegil** or **neerdan** (plural) }

I break or will break	agil nanu		
Thou breakest or wilt break	tegelaiiye	Break thou	tegella
He she or it breaks or will break	kegel nenye		
We break or will break	kegel iog		
You break or will break	anai igil	Break ye	endegi
They break or will break	kegel nenje		

Infinitive of **to dig** = **nashid, neturr** or **nairem**

I dig or will dig	atur nanu		
Thou diggest or wilt dig	tuturuiye	Dig thou	irotuturu
He she or it digs or will dig	ketuturo ninyi		
We dig or will dig	ketuturo siog		
You dig or will dig	anagetu	Dig ye	ainshom en- dudu
They dig or will dig	eturrninji		

Present or Future Tense   *Imperative Mood*

Infinitive of **to build** = **neegarr** or **nairau**

I build or will build	aitwa		
Thou buildest or wilt build	endawi	Build thou	daisherder
He she or it builds or will build	etaw ninyi		
We build or will build	kendaw iog		
You build or will build	anaiedaw	Build ye	endaishet
They build or will build	edaweninji		

Infinitive of **to fall** = **nebarr** or **nabarada**

I fall or shall fall	atabaradi		
Thou fallest or wilt fall	etabarad iye	Fall thou	tabararaio
He she or it falls or will fall	etabaradi ninyi		
We fall or shall fall	ketabaradadiog		
You fall or will fall	etabaradadandai	Fall ye	tabararaio
They fall or will fall	enaketabarada		

Infinitive of **to beg** = **namon** or **niomon**

I beg or will beg	monisho nanu		
Thou beggest or wilt beg	monisho iye	Beg thou	toomono
He she or it begs or will beg	monisho ninyi		
We beg or will beg	monisho iog		
You beg or will beg	monisho ndai	Beg ye	lāamonok
They beg or will beg	anakiomonisho		

Infinitive of **to blow** = { **nerr** or **neenok** (singular) / **negenok** (plural) }

I blow or will blow	togota nanu		
Thou blowest or wilt blow	togota iye	Blow thou	togota
He she or it blows or will blow	togotai nenye		
We blow or will blow	endokotiog		
You blow or will blow	endokotendai	Blow ye	endogot
They blow or will blow	endokotenenje		

2—2

Present or Future Tense   *Imperative Mood*

Infinitive of **to boil** = {**naitokitok** (singular)
{**negirri** (plural)

I boil or will boil	aitokitoki		
Thou boilest or wilt boil	etokitok iye	Boil thou	ēntokitoki
He she or it boils or will boil	etokitoki ninyi		
We boil or will boil	etokitoki siog		
You boil or will boil	etokitok ndai	Boil ye	ēntokitok
They boil or will boil	ketokitoki ninji		

Infinitive of **to bend** = {**nerriu** (singular)
{**negirriü** (plural)

I bend or will bend	togoromaiyo		
Thou bendest or wilt bend	agorroma iye	Bend thou	errogoyu
He she or it bends or will bend	agorroma nenye		
We bend or will bend	barragorramarra		
You bend or will bend	endogoramari	Bend ye	errogoyu
They bend or will bend	kegorroma nenje		

Infinitive of **to eat** = {**nanya** (singular)
{**neginyanda** (plural)

I eat or will eat	anya nanu		
Thou eatest or wilt eat	kinya iye	Eat thou	enossa
He she or it eats or will eat	kenya nenye		
We eat or will eat	kenya siog		
You eat or will eat	kenya ndai	Eat ye	enossa
They eat or will eat	{kenya nenje		
	oō nenje		
	enosseje		

Infinitive of **to drink** = **nawok** or **niog**

I drink or will drink	awok		
Thou drinkest or wilt drink	iok iye	Drink thou	toōgo
He she or it drinks or will drink	keyog nenye		
We drink or will drink	aiog iog		
You drink or will drink	ewogkiog ndai	Drink ye	endoōg
They drink or will drink	kewog nenje		

Present or Future Tense   *Imperative Mood*

Infinitive of **to tell** = $\begin{cases}\textbf{najogi} \text{ (singular)}\\ \textbf{negijoogi} \text{ (plural)}\end{cases}$

I tell or will tell	ajogi nanu		
Thou tellest or wilt tell	ijog iye	Tell thou	tiagi
He she or it tells or will tell	ejoge nenye		
We tell or will tell	kejog iog		
You tell or will tell	kejoginendai	Tell ye	tiagi
They tell or will tell	kejoginenje		

Infinitive of **to sing** = $\begin{cases}\textbf{neeran} \text{ (singular)}\\ \textbf{negerran} \text{ (plural)}\end{cases}$

I sing or will sing	arranў		
Thou singest or wilt sing	erran iye	Sing thou	tarranya
He she or it sings or will sing	kerranenye		
We sing or will sing	keteranassiog		
You sing or will sing	eterranyan ndai	Sing ye	endarrain
They sing or will sing	kerrai nenje		

Infinitive of **to put** = $\begin{cases}\textbf{nairagi} \text{ or } \textbf{nebi} \text{ (singular)}\\ \textbf{negiragi} \text{ (plural)}\end{cases}$

I put or will put	eragai nanu		
Thou puttest or wilt put	eragiye	Put thou	erāgi
He she or it puts or will put	erage nenye		
We put or will put	kerragissiog		
You put or will put	kerragai ndai	Put ye	erragē
They put or will put	kerragai nenje		

Infinitive of **to sit** = $\begin{cases}\textbf{nardon} \text{ (singular)}\\ \textbf{netornyi} \text{ (plural)}\end{cases}$

I sit or will sit	ator nanu		
Thou sittest or wilt sit	toronaiye	Sit thou	tordona
He she or it sits or will sit	keroranya nenye		
We sit or will sit	kiton iog		
You sit or will sit	andararan ndai	Sit ye	etordona
They sit or will sit	otonorto nenje		

Present or Future Tense   *Imperative Mood*

Infinitive of **to look** = { **naingora** or **neengorr** (singular)
{ **negengorr** (plural)

I look or will look	engor nanu		
Thou lookest or wilt look	engoraiye	Look thou	engorāīi
He she or it looks or will look	engora nenye		
We look or will look	keyaw } kengora } siog		
You look or will look	kengora ndai	Look ye	engorā
They look or will look	kengera nenje		

Infinitive of **to spit** = { **nenortargi** (singular)
{ **neginortagi** (plural)

I spit or will spit	tonortagi		
Thou spittest or wilt spit	etonortagiye	Spit thou	tonortargi
He she or it spits or will spit	ketonortag nenye		
We spit or will spit	kenotag iog		
You spit or will spit	enototargi ndai	Spit ye	tonortargi
They spit or will spit	enototargi nenje		

Infinitive of **to open** = { **nabol** or **nebol** (singular)
{ **negibol** (plural)

I open or will open	alag nanu		
Thou openest or wilt open	etalag iye	Open thou	{taala {tobollo
He she or it opens or will open	kalago nenye		
We open or will open	kelaguyoog		
You open or will open	elagalag ndai	Open ye	endala
They open or will open	keralagu nenje		

Infinitive of **to shut** = { **naigen** (singular)
{ **nigingin** (plural)

I shut or will shut	āteena		
Thou shuttest or wilt shut	ēen iye	Shut thou	teena
He she or it shuts or will shut	ēenenye		
We shut or will shut	ēen iog		
You shut or will shut	ēen ndai	Shut ye	endeen
They shut or will shut	ēenenje		

Present or Future Tense   *Imperative Mood*

Infinitive of **to stand** = {**naitashi** (singular)
{**negendaishi** (plural)

I stand or will stand	aitashu		
Thou standest or wilt stand	endaishu iye	Stand thou	endaishu
He she or it stands or will stand	kedaishe nenye		
We stand or will stand	kendaishiniog		
You stand or will stand	endasheshendai	Stand ye	endāishu
They stand or will stand	edashe nenje		

Infinitive of **to pull** = {**naiyeta** (singular)
{**negiyetu** (plural)

I pull or will pull	aiyetu		
Thou pullest or wilt pull	teyeraiye	Pull thou	teyerai
He she or it pulls or will pull	teyeraiy nenye		
We pull or will pull	kierai iog		
You pull or will pull	eteryeraiyendai	Pull ye	endeyerai
They pull or will pull	eteryeraiyenenje		

Infinitive of **to remove** = {**naidaw** or **nadomo** (singular)
{**negendaw** (plural)

I remove or will remove	adomo nanu		
Thou removest or wilt remove	idom iye	Remove thou {todomo {endaw	
He she or it removes or will remove	edomo nenye		
We remove or will remove	edom iog		
You remove or will remove	endodom ndai	Remove ye	endodomo
They remove or will remove	kerdomo nenje		

Infinitive of **to dance** = {**nengorran** (singular)
{**negigorran** (plural)

I dance or will dance	aigurran		
Thou dancest or wilt dance	ingurran iye	Dance thou	ingurrana
He she or it dances or will dance	engurran nenye		
We dance or will dance	engurran iog		
You dance or will dance	engorran ndai	Dance ye	engurran
They dance or will dance	kegorran nenje		

Present or Future Tense   *Imperative Mood*

Infinitive of **to swear** = $\begin{cases} \textbf{nadek} \\ \textbf{aadek} \\ \textbf{negedek} \end{cases}$ (singular)
(singular)
(plural)

I swear or will swear	amorr nanu		
Thou swearest or wilt swear	morr iye	Swear thou	tamoro
He she or it swears or will swear	kemorr nenye		
We swear or will swear	emorr iog		
You swear or will swear	emorromorr ndai	Swear ye	tamoro
They swear or will swear	kemorr nenje		

Infinitive of **to steal** = $\begin{cases} \textbf{neberro} \text{ (singular)} \\ \textbf{negibirro} \text{ (plural)} \end{cases}$

I steal or will steal	atuborrishi		
Thou stealest or wilt steal	etuburrushoiye	Steal thou	tuburroi
He she or it steals or will steal	etuburrushoi nenye		
We steal or will steal	ketuburrushi siog		
You steal or will steal	ketuburrisho ndai	Steal ye	enduburroi
They steal or will steal	keburrisho nenje		

Infinitive of **to hunt** = $\begin{cases} \textbf{nengorishu} \text{ (singular)} \\ \textbf{negingorishu} \text{ (plural)} \end{cases}$

I hunt or will hunt	angorisho		
Thou huntest or wilt hunt	engorishoiye	Hunt thou	angorrisho
He she or it hunts or will hunt	engorishoi nenye		
We hunt or will hunt	kengorishoi siog		
You hunt or will hunt	engorishoi ndai	Hunt ye	andangorr-isho
They hunt or will hunt	engorishoi nenje		

Present or Future Tense   *Imperative Mood*

Infinitive of **to refuse** = {**nian** or **ān** (singular)
{**negian** (plural)

I refuse or will refuse	aiin nanu	
Thou refusest or wilt refuse	een iye	Refuse thou taanya
He she or it refuses or will refuse	keenenye	
We refuse or will refuse	kiän siog	
You refuse or will refuse	ianiandai	Refuse ye endaān
They refuse or will refuse	keänenje	

Infinitive of **to forget** = {**nariginu** or **ireginu** (singular)
{**negeriginu** (plural)

I forget or will forget	atorigini nanu	
Thou forgettest or wilt forget	ekitorigin iye	Forget thou adorigin
He she or it forgets or will forget	ketorigine nenye	
We forget or will forget	etorigin iog	
You forget or will forget	etorigin ndai	Forget ye adorigin
They forget or will forget	etorigine nenje	

Infinitive of **to run away** = {**nilwaiyer** (singular)
{**negilwaiyer** (plural)

I run or will run away	aibirriyu	
Thou runnest or wilt run away	imbirr iye	Run away thou embirriu
He she or it runs or will run away	kebirri nenye	
We run or will run away	embiretu ossiog	
You run or will run away	embirridi ndai	Run ye away embirriu
They run or will run away	embirri nenje	

Infinitive of **to pour** = {**nabeg** (singular)
{**negibeg** (plural)

I pour or will pour	aisuagi	
Thou pourest or wilt pour	essuag iye	Pour thou tebega
He she or it pours or will pour	essuage nenye	
We pour or will pour	essuag issiog	
You pour or will pour	essuagi ndai	Pour ye endebega
They pour or will pour	essuagi nenje	

Present or Future Tense   *Imperative Mood*

Infinitive of **to milk** = {**nebegul** (singular)
{**negebegngul** (plural)

I milk or will milk	aleb nanu		
Thou milkest or wilt milk	eleb iye	Milk thou	talebo
He she or it milks or will milk	keleb nenye		
We milk or will milk	keleb iog		
You milk or will milk	elebeleb ndai	Milk ye	endaleb
They milk or will milk	keleb nenje		

Infinitive of **to lie** = {**nailejesho** (singular)
{**negilajishu** (plural)

I lie or will lie	eardelejare		
Thou liest or wilt lie	eardiyelejare	Lie thou	elejesho
He she or it lies or will lie	eardenenyelejare		
We lie or will lie	keardiog elejare		
You lie or will lie	eardindai elejare	Lie ye	elejesho
They lie or will lie	keardinenje lejare		

Infinitive of **to breed** = {**neishu** (singular)
{**negishu** (plural)

I breed or will breed	arnoda *or* itishu		
Thou breedest or wilt breed	ernortaiye	Breed thou	enorda
He she or it breeds or will breed	kernoda nenye		
We breed or will breed	kernodassiog		
You breed or will breed	enorda ndai	Breed ye	enorda
They breed or will breed	kernoda nenje		

Infinitive of **to suck** = {**nernag** (singular)
{**neginag** (plural)

I suck or will suck	anāk		
Thou suckest or wilt suck	nag iye	Suck thou	tarnag
He she or it sucks or will suck	kernag nenye		
We suck or will suck	kernag issiog		
You suck or will suck	kernag ndai	Suck ye	endarnag
They suck or will suck	kernagenenje		

Present or Future Tense		*Imperative Mood*

Infinitive of **to sew** = $\begin{cases}\textbf{naribeshu} \text{ (singular)} \\ \textbf{negerebeshu} \text{ (plural)}\end{cases}$

I sew or will sew	aribeshu nanu		
Thou sewest or wilt sew	aribeshu iye	Sew thou	tereba
He she or it sews or will sew	aribeshu nenye		
We sew or will sew	keribishiog		
You sew or will sew	ereberb ndai	Sew ye	enderibishu
They sew or will sew	eribishu nenje		

Infinitive of **to throw** = $\begin{cases}\textbf{nananga} \text{ (singular)} \\ \textbf{neginana} \text{ (plural)}\end{cases}$

I throw or will throw	erananga iyi		
Thou throwest or wilt throw	tanganaiye	Throw thou	tanganai
He she or it throws or will throw	keranganaiyi nenye		
We throw or will throw	keranganaitissiog		
You throw or will throw	eranganait ndai	Throw ye	endananga
They throw or will throw	eranganaiti nenje		

Irregular Verbs.

Infinitive of **to say** = $\begin{cases}\textbf{n\=ero} \text{ (singular)} \\ \textbf{negero} \text{ (plural)}\end{cases}$

I say or will say	etejo nanu		
Thou sayest or wilt say	nananorojo	Say thou	toojo
He she or it says or will say	erroijo		
We say or will say	kitaijai iog		
You say or will say	endai narijo	Say ye	endojo
They say or will say	anaketijo		

Infinitive of **to ask** = $\begin{cases}\textbf{negiligwena} \text{ (singular)} \\ \textbf{negingiligwan} \text{ (plural)}\end{cases}$

I ask or will ask	aigiligweno		
Thou askest or wilt ask	ingiligweanaiye	Ask thou	giligwena
He she or it asks or will ask	egiligwana		
We ask or will ask	kigiligwŭenutwa		
You ask or will ask	kigiligwŭeana ndai	Ask ye	engiligwena
They ask or will ask	anaingiliigwŭena		

Present or Future Tense   *Imperative Mood*

Infinitive of **to die** $=\begin{cases}\textbf{naii} \text{ or } \textbf{ää} \text{ (singular)} \\ \textbf{eyogee} \text{ (plural)}\end{cases}$

I die or shall die	aia nanu		
Thou diest or wilt die	ēeji	Die thou	etua
He she or it dies or will die	kee nenye		
We die or shall die	ekee iog		
You die or will die	kie ndai	Die ye	etua
They die or will die	ketwada ninji		

Infinitive of **to fight** $=\begin{cases}\textbf{naiirishu} \text{ or } \textbf{naarr} \text{ (singular)} \\ \textbf{negierishu} \text{ (plural)}\end{cases}$

I fight or will fight	ataara		
Thou fightest or wilt fight	etaarii	Fight thou	taara
He she or it fights or will fight	aataosho		
We fight or will fight	kitioshosidu		
You fight or will fight	etaara ndai	Fight ye	endaraada
They fight or will fight	etaarade nenje		

Verbs of Negation.

I can	aidim nanu
Thou canst	endem iye
He she or it can	kaidem nenye
We can	keendem iog
You can	kedem ndai
They can	kedem nenje

I cannot	maidim
Thou canst not	meedem
He she or it cannot	maidem nenye
We cannot	meedem iog
You cannot	meedem ndai
They cannot	meedem nenje

Present or Future Tense		*Imperative Mood*	
I do not or shall not like	manyorr		
Thou dost not or wilt not like	minyorr		
He she or it does not or will not like	menyorr ninyi		
We do not or will not like	mekinyorriyog		
You do not or will not like	menyorr ndai		
They do not or will not like	menyorr ninji		
I do not or will not wait	maanyo		
Thou dost not or wilt not wait	main iye	Wait not	mianyo
He she or it does not or will not wait	maanyo nenye		
We do not or will not wait	mitianyi yoog		
You do not or will not wait	mitianyo ndai	Wait ye not	emianyo
They do not or will not wait	miyu nenje nian-yuio		
I do not or will not eat	etu nananya		
Thou dost not or wilt not eat	etu nwananya	Eat not	emenyenda
He she or it does not or will not eat	etu nenjenye		
We do not or will not eat	etu siog enye		
You do not or will not eat	anaketu nanya	Eat ye not	emenya
They do not or will not eat	ketu nenjene		
I do not or will not drink	etu nanawok		
Thou dost not or wilt not drink	ketuyiwok	Drink not	emiog
He she or it does not or will not drink	ketwog nenye		
We do not or will not drink	etossiog iog		
You do not or will not drink	ketundai woki-woko	Drink ye not	emiog
They do not or will not drink	ketuog nenje		

Present or Future Tense   *Imperative Mood*

I do not or will not want	maiyu
Thou dost not or wilt not want	miyu
He she or it does not or will not want	meyu nenye
We do not or will not want	meyu iog
You do not or will not want	meyu ndai
They do not or will not want	meaw nenje

PHRASES.

Phrases of Negation.

I do not know	maiulu
I do not understand	etunanwaning or etoaning
I do not want	maiu
I will not go	etwaolo
I will not drink	etwaowok
I will not return	marrinyinyi or etwaininyi
I will not make	etu nainoreber
I do not want to go	maiyu nanunalo
I have not seen anything	etwa adoldogi
I do not like that man	maiu erreltungani
Not good	me sidai
Not bad	mer torono
No water	mer ngare
No food	mer nda
Not large	me kitok
He will not bring	eteau
You will not hear	eturenyi
We will not come	etiyu kibonu
They will not know	maiulo ninji
He will not say	etweja nenye
We will not drink	etu kiog
You are not old	meragitok
You have not seen anything	etuiye edoldogi
He has not seen me	etwadol nenye
We have not seen anyone	etiyo kidologonanyi
They have not seen me	etwadol ninji
We do not want to go	mikiieyu nigibu
They do not want to fight	miyau niarara
Do not bring food	meiaw nda
Do not bring water	meiaw ngare
We will not carry	etuyōger
Not this man, the other one	mereltungani, legai

Phrases of Interrogation.

What is your name?	kejinai ngarrana inu?
What is the time?	kabai ngolong? (lit. where is the sun?)
What are you doing?	ainyo endober?
What is this?	ainyena?
What do you want?	ainyoiyu?
What medicine do you want?	ainyo oldyani liū?
What news or what?	ainyo?
Why are you waiting?	ainyo erjano?
Where are you going?	kajiilu or ajilo?
Where is your sister?	kore anganashe ingu?
Where is the child?	kore ngerai?
Where do you come from?	kajingwaia?
Where is my knife?	kore olalim elai?
Why sleep?	ainyo berora or oberora?
Why eat?	ainyo begenoss?
Why drink?	ainyo beiok?
Why good?	ainyo basidai?
Why cry?	ainyo beenjirr?
Why dance?	ainyo begerran?
Why come?	ainyo belotu?
Why go?	ainyo belo?
Why I?	ainyo bananu?
Why he?	ainyo banenye?
Why meat?	ainyo bangirri?
What do you want to say?	ainyo iyu nēro?
Does he want to bring his child here?	eyu nerigu ngerai nyenne?
Do they want to return?	keyu nenje nerrinyu?
Do you want to return?	iyu iye nerrinyu?
Do they want to ask for anything?	kuyu nenje ngiligwena toki?
Does he want to see me?	eyu nenye nadol?
Do you want to see me?	iyu nadol iye?
Will you eat?	inossaiiye?

Phrases to illustrate the Infinitive Mood.

I want to go	aiyu nanu nalo
Do you want to come?	iyu nilotu?
Do you want to go?	iyu nilu?
They want to build a boma	keyu neegarr engang
He does not want to wait	meyu nuanyorr
I want to bathe	aiyu naisoja
I want to wake early	aiyu naiogi ainyorodo
I want to drink	aiyu nawog
I want to sleep	aiyu nairora
We want to bathe	iyu negasoja
I want to boil water	aiyu naitokitok ngare
Do they want to eat?	kiyu nenya?
We want to drink	iyu ngiog
I do not want to eat	maiyu nanya
We want to say	kiyu negero
I want to sit down	aiyu nardon
I want to look	aiyu nengora
Does he want to drink?	keyu nawok?
I want to hear	aiyu nanu nani
We want to fight	kiyu ngigerishu
I want to know	aiyu nanu naiulu
To eat now	nanya taada
I want to finish the work	aiyu naideba ingias
I want to call the child	aiyu naibot ngerai
He wants to climb the tree	eyu negent oldiani
We want to buy cows	kiyu neginyawng ngishu
He wants to cook the food	eyu neyerr nda
They want to clean the boma	keyu noor engang
They want to wait	keyu niānyu
We want to take away the things	kiyu iog naidaw ndogitin
You want to dance	iyu nengorran
We want to dance	kiyu negigorran
We want to hear	kiyu negining
I want to fight	aiyu naarr
We want to sing	kiyu negerran
They want to sit down	keyu nenje netornyi

We want to look	kiyu negongorr
They want to come	keyu nenye nebon
He wants to ask	eyu negiligwan
We want to bring food	kiyu iog negiaw nda
I want to come	aiyu nalotu
We want to know	kiyu iog negiolog
We want to give	kiyu negenjog
I want to carry my gun	aiyu nanab enduil lai
They want to finish work	keyu nedebai ngias
I want to laugh	aiyu nakweni
They want to call	keyu nenje nĕebot
I want to die	aiyu naii
He wants to buy goats	eyu nenyong ndari
We want to cook the food	kiyu negiyen nda
I want to clean the house	aiyu naorr ngaji
I want to wait	aiyu naanyo
They want to break stones	keyu neerdan ossoito
I want to dig a garden	aiyu nairem ngurruma
I want to build a house	aiyu nanu nairaw ngaji
He is going to beg	eyu nenye niomon
We want to put	kiyu negiragi
We want to spit	kiyu neginortagi
We want to steal meat	kiyu negibirro ngirri
I want to refuse	aiyu ān
They want to refuse	keyu nenje nian
You want to run away	eyu nilwaiyer
We want to run away	kiyu negilwaiyer
I want to pour out water	aiyu nabeg ngare
We want to pour out water	kiyu negibeg ngare
He wants to milk the cows	eyu nebegul ngishu
They want to milk the cows	keyu negibegngul ngishu
He is going to hunt	eyu nengorishu
We want to hunt	kiyu iog negingorishu
I want to forget	aiyu nariginu
I want to sew	aiyu naribeshu
We want to sew	kiyu negerebeshu
She is going to breed	eyu neishu

Phrases in the First Person Singular.

I am cold	aning ingijāpi
I am hot	airogua nalin
I am hungry	aralameu
I am ill	aemwi
I am angry	ābe
I am going to the coast	alogisho kishwaiini
I am making medicine	aisholdyani
I am very ill	aemwi ossupati
I am going yonder	aloiiti
I am well	aishwosa nanu
I am old	nanu kitok
I drink milk	awokule
I am good	ara supatt
I am afraid	awuri
I want water	aiyu ngare
I want medicine	aiyu oldyani
I have called the man	aideba aibōdo eltungani
I have a stomach-ache	aia ngoshogi
I will eat	anyanda
I will bring food now	aiaw taada nda
I will shoot	alaara
I have made medicine	aideba endobera oldyani
I will give you food	aiisho nanu nda
I hear a noise	atoringu oibilebelebebe
I will kill the cow	aiyeng ngiting
I will return	arrinyinyi
I have slept long	airora osupati
I want more water	aiyu aiare
I want more milk	aiyu gulele
I want more meat	aiyu gulēgirri

Phrases to illustrate the Possessive.

I have a spear	aad eremet
I have a child	aadang ngerai
I have a father*	aada baba

* The words father (*baba*) and mother (*yeyu*) in Masai are only used by children with reference to their own parents: it is considered both unlucky and insulting to address the parents of others in these terms. When referring to the parents of other people, the terms *minyi* or *menye* are used for father, and *ngutungy, ngotongy, nutun* or *notorn* for mother.

I have a mother*	aara nanu yeyu
You (sing.) have a shield	eeta elongo
You (sing.) have a child	ere ngerai
You (sing.) have a father*	errai eminyi
You (sing.) have a mother*	errai ngutungy
He has a sword	eerda nenye olalim
He has a child	err ngerai iye
He has a father*	erra menye
We have spears	ker erremeta
We have no children	miker ngera
We have a father	kerrai iloababa
You (pl.) have swords	erra ndai lalima
You (pl.) have children	erra ndai ngera
You (pl.) have a father*	erra ndai minyi
They have spears	erra nenj erremeta
They have no children	merra nenje ngera
They have a father*	erra menye
My child	ngeraiē
My children	ngeraiini
My hand	ngaiinai
My bottle	oldulelai
My bag	orbenelai
My father	babalai
My mother	yeyulai
Your (sing.) father*	minyeli
Your (sing.) mother*	ngutungyi
Your (sing.) child	ngeraiino
Your (sing.) spear	erremetino
His father*	minyiye
His mother*	ngotongiye
His gun	endiulenye
His sister	nganashenye
Our father	baba elang
Our mother	yeyoōg
Our children	ngerang
Our cows	ngishuung
Our boma	engangang
Your (pl.) father*	minyi linyi
Your (pl.) mother*	nutun inyi
Your (pl.) dog	orldia linyi

* See footnote, page 35.

Your (pl.) skins	oljoni linyi
Their mother*	notornenye
Their house	engajenye
Their medicine	oljanienye
Their father*	minyenye or menye

Phrases to illustrate the Imperative.

Pour out a little more water	tebeg ngiti aiare
Bring drinking water	iaw ngare nau
Make a fire	inua ngima
Boil the water	endogodogi ngare
Call the man	embooto eltungani
Be quiet	endegerrara
Go away	inno
Come here	woo enne
Bring food	iaw nda
Put it outside	eragīri bo
Bring hot water	iaw ngare nairogua
Look or come here	ēro
Get out of the way	ewanga or engirriu
Go with me	maabe ooje
Make medicine	endobera oldyani
Wait for me	tainyogi
Take away the food	todomu nda
Tell the woman to come here	tiagi engitok oo enne
Tell me the truth	tolliigiogi supati
Wake me early	nenyegi taadagenia
Open the door	tobollo kutugaji
Shut the door	ingieno kutugaji
Give me water	enjoogi ngare
Come back soon	inoberininyi
Do not return	merrinyinyi
Bring more food	iaw iaida or eatatai
Take the things away	endaw ndogitin
Bring more men	torrigu kelogaitungana
Bring more children	torrigu gulegera
Bring more cows	terriaw gulegishu

* See footnote, page 35.

Bring more cold water	iaw aiare nairobi
Bring more chairs	iaw orrigaiishi
Bring more bottles	iaw illigaidulet
Give me milk	enjoogi nanugule
Give me meat	enjoōg ngirri
Give me food	enjoogi nda
Give me more milk	enjoogi guliele
Give me more meat	enjoogi gulēgirri

Phrases.

A big boy	sabuk orlaion
A big child	ngerai bordorr
A big woman	engitok sabuk
The boys are bad	egogong elaiyoik
The men are good	supati korlungana
The lions are fierce	inossisho logwaru
A long house	ērdo ngāiiji
A black goat	ndari narok
Many black goats	kumuk ndari nārok
A red cow	ngiting ainyuki
Many red cows	ngishu nyainyuki kumuk
A stupid woman	ershall ngorrion
Stupid women	ershall kenangorriok
A bad man	egogo eltungani
Bad men	egogo orrltungana
A strong horse	ebē mbarrda
Strong horses	ebē mbarrdan
The child has gone	eshomo ngerai
The children have gone	eshomo ngera
The man has come	ewar eltungani
The men have come	ietu eldongana
A big man	eltungani sabuk
Two big men	sabuki orrldongana ari
Four good children	supati konengera ungwun
Five large cows	sabuki ngishu miet
Three good women	sidai engitua ooni
A big donkey	sabuk issigerria
Big donkeys	sabuki ollissirrgon
How much?	kaija?

To give gratis	aishu apeshu
I say	īya
To express thanks	kitaritu
To make a noise	obilebelēbebe or elebeleb
Are you ill?	imwe?
How many men are there here?	kaija eltungana enne?
The rain is near	eteana ngai
You are dirty	eata olaireriu
How many eggs are there here?	kaija mossorr enne?
Are you tired?	eji enawri
It will rain in the night	ewar ngai kawarie
They are all going	eshomo bōōgi
This smells bad	ellele
The wind is strong	aikitok ollimwa
The wind is not strong	mekitok ollimwa
The clothes are wet	aishai ngelani
There are forty zebras	eti loidugoi arrtam
I have seen thirty-one congoni	arradu orrgorigori ossom oobo
I have seen a hundred cows	arradua ngishu ip
There are fifteen goats here	eti enne ndari tomonoimiet
You have told a lie	edegwela elejere
The journey is long	kitok ennasapari
You have stolen my goats	etuburoi ndariai
You go to-day	ilo taada
You have gone	edeba shomo
In a little while	errongonongon or kiti kweji
We want to drink	kiju iog nkiog
You have seen ten children	ertadua ngera tomon
We have seen many children	erradua ngera kumuk
More rain is coming	ewar aii
Under the trees	abori oljani
They have made a big war	etobera engitok weji
They are having a big dance	eti ngigorau edeweji
We will go for a walk	kibeba aileleta
He is coming	nyelolutu
You and I will go out	kibwa ellela alileta
The dog and cat are friends	enoyr oldia mbarrie
You and I	nanoiye
The dog and cat	orldia embarrie
The man and woman	eltungana engitok
The sheep and goats	ngerr engini
The cows and goats	ngishu ordari
You and he	nenyoiye

You are angry	egogo iye
He is old	atakitok
We are afraid	kiewre
You (pl.) are foolish	emadada ndai
He is bad	serrseri
You (sing.) are good	eraiye supatt
He is good	sidai nenye
He is hungry	erda lameŭ
You (sing.) are hungry	etala meŭ
We are good	kera sidan
We are old	kera dasat
We are hungry	kera lameŭ
They are good	sidanenje
They are old	morruanenje
They are afraid	arraiure

SALUTATIONS.

Salutation to a woman (literally "laugh")	tagwenia
,, ,, ,, (plural)	tagwenia bōōgi
Reply	īgo
To a man	soboi
Reply	eber
On shaking hands	nassak

Song the children sing for rain.

Siumbi aielisiumbi ngai kijaiga eo!
God we sing, God rain we pray thee oh!

Medicine Song.

Aamon yi ngai, aamon m'Batian.
We pray God, we pray Batian.

Song sung by the warriors when going to fight Sendeyo.

Sendeyo manoloimoti tendeboi errakenja bonik oldash irremeta.

Sendeyo has done evil, we were friends once but now we go to fight him with our spears, the big ones in front, the small behind.

	Orrmāssani	Singular of Masai	
	elmāsai	Plural of Masai	
Hunters	{ olldōrrobon	Singular	
	{ dōrrobo	Plural	
Iron workers	{ orrgunoni	Singular	
	{ elgunonu	Plural	

Kenia (mt.)	oldonyo gēri (the striped mountain)
Kilima Njaro (mt.)	oldonyo eborr (the white mountain)
Suswa (mt.)	oldonyo kenyuki (the red mountain)
Nairobi (river)	Cold (the river comes from the forest and is very cold as it emerges into the open)
Ngongo bagas (river)	(the eye of the Spring)
Eldonyo sabuk (mt.)	(the big mountain)
Gwasso kidong (river)	the river of the ollokidong trees (the wood of these trees is used for making quivers)
Enaibasha (lake)	the great water or sea

Curses.

Djerrterrā	A curse against the man addressed
Njertērrda	Against the man addressed
Mining jangayenda	Against a man and his father
Kirrigūmini	A curse on the father saying the person cursed is a bastard
Injeraii	This curse is supposed to cause the death of a brother or sister
Tadui munigilidoigi	This curse is supposed to cause the person addressed to die
Injerai kordai	A child's curse
Miinjirria nigiruk	A child's curse
Mbussa bwaara	Fool
Mbarra	This is accompanied by spitting and is the equivalent of damn

VOCABULARY

A

abdomen (lower)	enganoiri
acacia (wild)	osseneyer
across (water)	talanga
adjoining	ertasha
adjudge* (v. Imp.)	tudungu orrori (literally, to cut the noise or difficulty)
adulteress	kiborrong
afraid	awure gurede
afternoon	engeberada ngolong
afterwards	tengai, āde
again	enagi
ahead	nologonya
alive	bīōtu
all	bōōgi
all of us	iō bōōgin
allow (v. Imp.)	aishöilu
all right	aiya
aloe	oldoboi
alone	nanu wake (literally, I alone)
also	oshiagi
alter (v. Imp.)	imenejengo
always	engolong ebōōgi (literally, all days or suns)
angry	abe, ebi
ankle	olloregogoiyu pl. loirigegiru
anklets (of skin)	emonge pl. mmongen
answer (v. Imp.)	tedema
ant (large black)	olloisuisui

* All the verbs have been given in the Imperative, as well as many in the Infinitive mood, since it is possible, before mastering the conjugations, to make oneself understood in Masai by using the Imperative Mood only. It is, therefore, important that the Imperatives should be learnt first.

ant (small black)	engalāū
ant (red, siafu)	emuyu pl. muyu
ant (white)	orriri pl. irriai
antelope	engoili pl. engōīlin
anything	toki
apace	enguerrara
arm (the whole)	ngaina pl. ngaieg
arm (fore)	endagūle pl. endagūlin
arm (upper)	orberangash pl. elberangashi
armpit	ngitīgiti pl. ngitigit (literally, tickle)
arrive (v. Imp.)	kerabaaidi
arrow	embai pl. embā
ashes	ngurruwun pl. ngurruwun
ask (v. Imp.)	engīligwena, ngiligwena (Infin.)
at once	taada
awake (v. Imp.)	inyo
axe	endōlu pl. endōluĕr

B

baboon	olldōlal pl. olldolalli
back	engorriong pl. engōrriong
back (small of)	ollōro pl. olloroom
bad	egogong (animate objects)
bad	torono (inanimate objects)
bag	orrbeni pl. elebeni
banana	elmaisuri pl. olmaisuri
baobab tree	ollimisera
barb (of arrow)	essebil pl. essebilli
bark (v. Imp.)	tabua
bark (of tree)	engabobook pl. engabobook
barrenness	olupi mer engera
basket*	engiondo (kikuyu) pl. engiondoni
bastard	engerai orlatolac (literally, child of dirt)
bathe (v. Imp.)	aisojai {naisoja (sing.) negasoja (pl.)} Infin.
beads	mussitani or osain pl. essain
beak	ollororom pl. ollororom
beard	orrimünyi pl. orrimünyi

* The Masai have no word for basket, and make use of the Kekuyu word.

because	aiinyo
bed	erruat pl. erruati
bee	oltoroki pl. lodorok
beer (native)	enjoii
beetle	orromwila pl. elmwiela
beg (v. Imp.)	toomonu, namon (Infin.)
beggar	orlāmonon pl. lāmonok
belch	olljerādi
bell (small)	enduela pl. endwalan
bell (cow)	engorrogorr pl. engorrogorru
bell (warrior's)	oldwalan pl. eldwalan
bellows	engune pl. engunēi
belt	ingitadi pl. inkitadin
bend (v. Imp.)	torrigu $\begin{cases} \text{nerriu (sing.)} \\ \text{negirriü (pl.)} \end{cases}$ Infin.
better	ishigo, ingiwa
between	porrloss
bird	ndaridigi pl. ndāridig
birds (small)	engelloguny
bite (v. Imp.)	toonyo, erronyo, nawon (Infin.)
bitter	edua
black	erok
bladder (urinal)	orrgulet pl. orrgulet
blade (of knife)	essibirr orlalim
blade (of spear)	essibirr
blaze (v.)	orlangal
blind person	mordon pl. elmodon
blood	assarge
blow nose (v.)	enduyuro guluk
blow (v. Imp.)	tokodar, neenok (Infin.)
blue	mbusth ollonyori
boat	etawalānget
body	ossesi pl. essessin
bog	earsurr pl. earsurr
boil (v. Imp.)	endogidogi or etokitok, naitokitok (Infin.)
boma (zariba)	engang pl. engangiti
bone	oloiitu pl. loiik
boot	enamoki pl. namoka
border	erreshata
bore (v. Imp.)	tarremo
born (v.)	nitoiishi (Infin.)
both	bogirari (literally, all two)
bottle	oldulet pl. olduleta

bow	ngaw pl. ngaii
boy	orlaiyon pl. laiyok
boy (little)	laiyōnigiti
bracelet	orgatā pl. elkatari
brain	ollālogonia or ollaibrinyi pl. ollaibrinyinyi
branch	engossela pl. enlenōssel
break (v. Imp.)	tegēlla, negil (Infin.)
breast	orrigena pl. ellgiē
breed (v. Imp.)	erroishi, neishu (Infin.)
bridge	orlanget pl. langerta
bring (v. Imp.)	iaw, negiaw (Infin.)
bring forth (about to)	endua
broad	dabash
broom	alāraw pl. alārawon
brother	ollalashe pl. ollalashera
brother-in-law	olabadani pl. elabatak
buffalo	alāru pl. elāroii
build (v. Imp.)	engarra or desherder, nairaw (Infin.)
bull	orlōīngoni pl. orlaingok
burn (v. Imp.)	eēka
burr	enderrobenyi
bury (v. Imp.)	tornoga
bush buck	ollbua
bustard (great)	kūgogēli
bustard (lesser)	orrgēlababa pl. ellgerralababa
but	kaki
butter	engorrno pl. engorrn
butterfly	ossamburubui pl. samburuburu
buttocks	ollduli, ollgorom
buy (v. Imp.)	enyāngu $\begin{Bmatrix} \text{nenyong (sing.)} \\ \text{neginawng (pl.)} \end{Bmatrix}$ Infin.
by myself	nanu waki or wagi
by thyself	iyagi
by himself	ninyagi
by ourselves	iogagi
by yourselves	ndaiagi
by themselves	eninjagi

C

calf	olashi pl. olasho
calf (of leg)	olldiim
call (v. Imp.)	embōotu or emborru, naibot (Infin.)

camel	ndamess pl. ndarmessi. ngaiurr
cap	engarranda pl. engãrranda
captain	ollaigwanan pl. laigwanak
carross	engela nderr (literally, clothes of sheep)
carry (v. Imp.)	tanabo. nanab (Infin.)
cartridges	ossoiit lendiul (literally, stones of the gun)
castrate (v. Imp.)	egellema
cat	erongo or mbãrrie pl. mbarria
catch (v. Imp.)	emboonga. {nebong (sing.)} {negibong (pl.)} Infin.
caterpillar	ollogurrto pl. ollogurrt
cat tribe	logwãru pl. logwãrak
cause	endiaragi
centipede	ossambela pl. ossambelali
central	enadoagada
chain	ollbīsiai pl. illbissia
chains (in ears)	emōnai pl. emōna
chains (for brass earrings)	illgorēda
chair	olōrika pl. lorrigaishi
chameleon	nottorrangi pl. nottorrangi
cheek	endagola pl. endagol
chest	orgoo, orgon pl. elgoon
chest (middle)	olludua
chew (tobacco)	enyalo orrgumbaw
chew (the cud)	enyang amura
chicken	elũgungu pl. elugunguni
chief	orlebon pl. oiloiboni
child	ngerãī pl. ngerã
chin	ollomoon or orboōn
chirp (v. Imp.)	eoritu
choose (v. Imp.)	kaiyuatagona
circle	eborogoran
circumcise (v. Imp.)	ermorrata
claws	oloisodo pl. loisoidok
clay	esserangap
clean	ēborr
clean (v. Imp.)	essoja, naorr (Infin.)
clematis (wild)	engorrōgi
clever	ebi or ertangainyel
climb (v. Imp.)	tagedo, negid (Infin.)
cloth	engelã pl. engelanī
cloth (warrior's war)	enanga
clothes	engelani

cloud	engarrambui pl. engarrambo
coast	enaibasha (literally, the great sea)
cold	ngijābi or erobi
cold (in head)	ebissēnga
collar	emāīrai pl. mmāīita
colobus monkey	orrgorroi pl. ellgorroien
colour	serret
come (v. Imp.)	ōōtuōō or wōō, nalolu or nebo (Infin.)
come back (v. Imp.)	torrininyi or torrinyo
conceal (v. Imp.)	essudōīi
conceive	ernöda or erreingu ngerai
conquer (v. Imp.)	eturrua
cook (v. Imp.)	tiarra. {neyerr (sing.)} {negiyerr (pl.)} Infin.
cooking vessel	emoti pl. motiu
copulate (v.)	nenjoōgi ngumu (Infin.)
cord	engeenda pl. engeenda
cotton	embitu pl. embit
cough	engerroget
count (v. Imp.)	engēena
country	ngop pl. ngop
cover (v. Imp.)	tebessenga
cow	ngetēlibong, ngiting (head of cattle) pl. ngishu
cow-killing house	ollobul pl. ellbuli
coward	gurede pl. gurede
cowry	ossegerai pl. essegera
crab	essurusuri
crawl (a man)	eerberebarri
creep (an animal)	essberbarri
crested crane	enaitoli pl. enaitolia
cricket	surūsurī
crocodile	orrgenōss pl. ergenossin
crow (white necked)	orgorrok pl. elgūrruki
crow (v. Imp.)	eoritu
crush (v. Imp.)	erronya
cry (v. Imp.)	isheera or injeera. neenjerr (Infin.)
cup (drinking vessel)	orrbugurri
cure	esshivo
custom	supatt (literally, what is good)
cut (v. Imp.)	tudungu {nadung (sing.)} {negidung (pl.)} Infin.

D

dance	ingiguran pl. maigurana
dance (v.)	{nengorran (sing.) {negigorran (pl.) } Infin.
dark	enaimen
dawn	etawanga or engagenia
day	ngolong pl. ngolong
day after to-morrow	ngaiolong
daylight	dāma
dead body	etuer
deaf	etwani
dear (price)	ergol
deep	orrmoti
deny (v. Imp.)	enjangārr
dew	engoileli
diarrhoea	equet ngoshogi (literally, running away of the stomach)
dic-dic	essūni pl. essūni
die (v. Imp.)	etua. naii (Infin.)
difficult	ergol
dig (v. Imp.)	tuduru
dirt	olloieriyu or orlatolac
dirty	essūd
disembowel (v. Imp.)	tadanya ngoshogi
divide (v. Imp.)	endorr
dog	orldia pl. eldiain
donkey (female)	ossigirria pl. issirrgŏn
donkey (male)	olāmwe pl. ellamweishi
door	kutugaiji pl. engutuengaijik
do you hear	ēji or etoningu
draw (water) (v.)	ndogua ngare (Infin.)
dream	aideridet
drink (v. Imp.)	tooko, niog or nawok (Infin.)
drive away (v. Imp.)	temerra
drum	ossingoilu pl. ossingoilu
drunk (to be)	etemerre
duck	emotorroki pl. emotorok
dumb	erebogotok
dung (cow's)	emodue pl. modiok
dust	enderit
dust storm	ollimwa
duyker (antelope)	mparnass pl. mparnass

E

eagle	ormotonyingeru pl. ormotonyingeroi
ear	engiok pl. ingīā
ear (animal's)	menēss
ear (lobe)	essegerrua
ear (top edge)	orrgedebet
ear (hole in lobe)	essēgerrua
early	taadagenia or peiko
early (very)	taiku
earring	essurutie pl. essorudia
earwig	engolōpa
easy	endobera nagititogi (literally, doing small things)
eat (v. Imp.)	inosa, nanya (Infin.)
egg	emossorri pl. emosorr
egret	enarrlēli
eight	issiet
eighteen	tomonoissiet
eight times	katitin issiet
eland	ossiriwa pl. issīrriwai
elbow	ollaidolol pl. öiloidolloli
elder	elbaiyen kitok
elephant	eldonyroirosabuk pl. eldanga sabuki or elangaiina or oldome
elephant grass	ollgerrionn
eleven	tomononabu
end	ebaiyi
endure (v. Imp.)	tegeraiye mero
enemy	ormangatinda pl. elmargati
entrails	embulati
equal	errisüi
Europe	geshuaini
every	bōōgi
everything	edogiding bōōgi
evil eye	egurrtoōng or possongu
exchange	mataorlage
eye	ngongo pl. ngonyek
eyebrows } eyelashes }	elbabit ngongo (literally, the hairs of the eyes)
eyelid (upper)	shomata ngong (the roof of the eye)
eyelid (lower)	abori ngong (under the eye)
eye (pupil of)	nerok ngoug (the black of the eye)
eye (white of)	eborr ngong (the white of the eye)

F

face	ngomom pl. ngomom
faint	olloididua
fall (v. Imp.)	erabaradi. nebarada (Infin.)
far	orelagua or elakwa
fast	tässiogi
father	baba
father-in-law	bagerr
father-in-law (who gives cows)	bageten
feather	ingobirri pl. ngobirr
feed (cattle, v. Imp.)	erreda
female	ngitok pl. ngituak
female (term of opprobrium)	ngoiraiyon pl. ngoirroiok
fifteen	tomon oimiet
fifty	orrnom
fight (v. Imp.)	etaara $\begin{cases} \text{naar (sing.)} \\ \text{negigerishu (pl.)} \end{cases}$ Infin.
fig-tree (wild)	olloboni
fill (v. Imp.)	eborri
find (v. Imp.)	erradua
finger	orkimojinu pl. irrkimojik
finger (1st)	sagurishe
finger (2nd)	olgeredi
finger (4th)	ingilinda
finish (v. Imp.)	edebi or tabala, naideba (Infin.)
fir-cone	ollmoror
fire	ngima pl. ngima
firewood	elgēg
fish	ossengeri pl. essengerr
fish-bones	orgigui (lit. thorns)
fist	endololong ngaiina (the shut hand)
five	emiet
five times	kataimiet
flea	loisusu pl. loisusu
flour	engūrruma
flower	ndābogai pl. ndaboga
fly	ellojonga pl. ellojonga
fly (v. Imp.)	eēda or ebido, nebirr (Infin.)
fold (v. Imp.)	teena, neyen or ngened (Infin.)
foliage	mbenek

follow (v. Imp.)	tossoja
food	ndā pl. ndaiigi
fool	emwāda pl. emwāda
foot	ngaju pl. ngaijek
forehead	ngomom pl. ngomom
forest	endim pl. indimi
forget (v. Imp.)	adorigin, ariginu (Infin.)
forty	arrtam
four	ungwun
fourteen	tomon ungwun
four times	kat ungwun
friend	oldyore pl. eldjorduweta
frog	endua pl. enduan
froth	olabara
frown	issot ngomom
fruit	erangnaiyu or olongaboili
full	epotā or ebotā
furnace	orrgoguet

G

game (alive)	ngwess pl. ngwessi
game (meat)	ingēringu
game trap	orrgerenget
garden	ngurruma
gather (v. Imp.)	tadotu
gazelle (Grant's)	orrgwārragas pl. orrgwārragassi
gazelle (Thompson's)	engobera pl. engoobera
gentle	enana
get (v. Imp.)	inodo or anordo
get ahead	togiroii
get into	tejenagi
get out of the way	ingerriu
ghost	essicati eltungani
giddy	amana elogonya
giraffe .	oladōgaragat pl. eladorugeraget
girl	nairo or endoiyi pl. ndito
girl (little)	nditogiti
give (v. Imp.)	enjōōgi $\begin{cases} \text{nenjog (sing.)} \\ \text{negenjog (pl.)} \end{cases}$ Infin.
give chase	etemera
give trouble	ketelamana

glad	eshēba
glitter	elio
gnaw (v. Imp.)	tanyāala
go (v. Imp.)	shomo, nalo (Infin.)
go after	etosoja
go away (from a place)	edora
go bad	errarrui
go round	tamanāī
go together	endorobara
goat	ndari pl. ndāri
goat (castrated)	orrgini pl. engineji
goat (female)	ingine pl. ingineti
goat (female before bearing young)	essuben pl. essubeni
goat (male)	orlōrro pl. orlorroi
god	ngai pl. ngai
good	sidai
good (very)	āīiya
gourd	embuguri pl. embugurrtu
gradually	aketi
grandparent	ngaguya
grass	engojeta pl. engojet
grasshopper	endargēeti pl. endarrgēet
gratis	peshu
grave	engumoto
graze (v. Imp.)	ärda
great	sabuk
greedy	eūlu
green	ainyori
grey	mbusth or gwarigoi
grey hairs	eborr elogonya (white head)
grief	ossomet
ground	ngop or enguluguk
grow (v. Imp.)	etubulwa
growl	aigurrugurru
guard	orribi
guinea-fowl	orrgerisure pl. elgerrisurreni
gums	enyerrt
gums (at side)	eldagiligil
gun	endiul pl. endioli
guts	mainyet

H

hair	olbabeta pl. elbabit
half	ematua
hammer	orrgirrisiet
hand	ndap pl. ndapi
hand (palm of)	ndap ngaiina
hang (on wall, v. Imp.)	tolluwa
hasten (v. Imp.)	tassiogi guerder
hate (v. Imp.)	aiba
hawk	ollābebu pl. ollābebu
haze	errogenia
he	nenye
head	elogonya pl. elogŏn
head-dress (lion skin)	ollogwaru
head-dress (ostrich feathers)	engurraru pl. engurraruni
hear (v. Imp.)	atorningu $\begin{cases}\text{nani (sing.)}\\ \text{negining (pl.)}\end{cases}$ Infin.
heart	ōldaw pl. eldawaja
heavy	irruishi
hedgehog	enjōliss
heel	enduduniu pl. eududun
heifer	endāwu
herd	olljogut pl. eljoguti
here	enne
hiccup	engioget
hide (v. Imp.)	essudoii
hill	olosho pl. oiloishon
hippopotamus	ollōmagaw pl. errmagawl
his	enenye
hole	engūmoto pl. engumōt
honey	enaishu pl. enaiishi
honey box	engidong pl. ingidong
hongo	endau olmorrossi
hoof	oloisodŏk pl. oloisōdok
horn	emoworr pl. emowarrak
hornbill	orrgimasäja pl. elgemasajanan
horse	mbarrda pl. mbarrdan
house	ngaji pl. ngajijik
how many?	keraja or kaija
hump	errok pl. erroga

hungry	olamei
hunt (v. Imp.)	ngorrori $\begin{Bmatrix} \text{nengorishu (sing.)} \\ \text{negingorishu (pl.)} \end{Bmatrix}$ Infin.
husband (my)	elmōrrualai
hush	endegerata
hyæna	olnojeni pl. engorjin

I

I	nanu
ibis	momēra
ibis (black)	engalite
idle	ershall
ill	emwi
impala (antelope)	ndaragwet or ollolubu pl. ndaragweti
in	atua
infect	etasuroii
in front	nologonya
inherit	ejūngore
inside	etiaatwa
instead	inoitabaiidi
iron	essegēngi
iron-sand	senyāī

J

jackal	mbarrie pl. mbarria
jigger*	ndudu (kiswahili)
journey	enaidora pl. enaidorak
jump (v. Imp.)	olloiidi
juniper	ndaragwa

K

keep (v. Imp.)	shomorribie
kidney	ellairauguji pl. ellairaugut
kill (v. Imp.)	teyanga, neyeng (Infin.)

* The jigger was introduced among the Masai by the Swahilis, and the Masai describe it by the kiswahili word "insect."

kiss	atoŋgurtuda
kite	orrgillili pl. illgillilin
knee	engōngo pl. engong
knee hollow	endango pl. endangon
kneel (v. Imp.)	tegelāiigo
knife	olalim pl. olalema
knife (small)	engalimgiti
knife-handle	enjerdalalim
knob-kerry	orrguma pl. ellguman
knob-kerry (royal)	onguma lessegenggai
knock (v. Imp.)	engōoro
know (v. Imp.)	eeolo or iolu $\begin{cases} \text{naiulu (sing.)} \\ \text{negiolog (pl.)} \end{cases}$ Infin.
knuckles	errobāt irrkimojik
kudu	emālo pl. miggibu
kudu (lesser)	engimossorok

L

lame	ňgojēni
language	orroē
large	sabuk
last	korom
laugh (v. Imp.)	atagwenia, or engwenia $\begin{cases} \text{nakweni (sing.)} \\ \text{negigwena (pl.)} \end{cases}$ Infin.
lazy	ershall
lean (v. Imp.)	toshomagi essendai
lean on (v. Imp.)	tanāba
leave (v. Imp.)	tabala
leaves	imeriu
left hand	kediene
leg	ollōreshet pl. lorresheti
leopard	ologwarugeri pl. ologwarakerin
let go	tāla
lichen	narēro
lid	essīöti
lie	ellejore
lift (v. Imp.)	todomu, or elebi
light	ētegenia (no mist)
lightning	ewunger ŋgai
like (v. Imp.)	ainyorr $\begin{cases} \text{naanya (sing.)} \\ \text{negenyorr (pl.)} \end{cases}$ Infin.

like this	aneena
line	orgerrat
line (boundary)	erreshata ungwapi
lion	ŏlonătring pl. elnatungyu
lips	enjionengotok
liquid	elebeck
liver	emoinuar
lizard	olloirüri pl. ollairēri
load	olola pl. ololan
locust	olomădi pl. ellemäät
long	ērdo
long ago	ŏpa
look (v. Imp.)	engorāīi {naingora (sing.)} {negongorr (pl.)} Infin.
loose	meenussibari
lose (v. Imp.)	emena
lungs	orrgibie pl. irrigibiu

M

mad	ollaididua
maggot	illguru
magic	orgoiyatik pl. elgoīyatiki, or orjanga
maize	ellibaiak
make (v. Imp.)	endobera, nerobera (Infin.)
make love	aiju
male	ōlē pl. elēwa
man	eldungani pl. eldongana
man (old)	elmōrrua pl. lemorruak
many	kumuk
many times	nkatitin kumuk
marabout stork	enădogos pl. enădogossi
mark	orrborrnoto pl. irrgonot
marriage	enango engitok
marrow	endōlit pl. endōlo
marry (v. Imp.)	engabūdi, or endobera engabudi
mash (v. Imp.)	tegēlla
me	nanu
measure (v. Imp.)	tedema
meat	ingēringu, or engerri
medicinal herb (purge)	oldīmigom
medicine	oldyani

medicine man	ollibaiyon or orlaibon
melt (v. Imp.)	ilangalanga
mid-day	enaibirri ngolong
middle	engabe
milk	ngŭlē
milk (v. Imp.)	talebo, nebegul (Infin.)
mimosa (white)	llerrāiyi pl. lērra
mimosa (yellow)	enjorrāīyi
miscarriage	etaherwehi
mist	errogenia
money	engosholoi
mongoose	ollgorroi, or ollbeliss
monkey	engema pl. engemai, or naiokotok
month	elaba pl. elabaitin
moon	elaba pl. elabaitin
moon (new)	emoelaba
moon (day before full)	olgādet
moon (full)	olloinyon
moon (day after full)	olloinyuki (red moon)
more	guli or elang
morning	taadagenia
mosquito	engojonganye
mother	yeyu pl. noiyeyu
mother-in-law	bagerr
mountain	eldōinyo pl. eldoinyo or oldonyo
moustache	orrimünyi pl. orrimünyi
mouth	ngukuk, ngotuk pl. ngutuki
mud	eserrengap
muscle	ossēni, or sinigi
mushroom	labai
mutilate (v. Imp.)	endaruyi
my	enai or elai
myself	eranāīi, enaben, olloben

N

nails (finger)	loisōdök
nails (brass, etc.)	olldedu
naked	merengela (no clothes)
name	ngārrana pl. ngärrana
narrow	rongāī

navel	ossororia
near	eteana
neck	emurrt pl. emurrtu
neck, nape of	essangurigili
necklace	enorrini pl. enorrin
necklace (beads and long iron chains)	ollōmutu
necklace (beads and short iron chains)	ngāīshu
necklace (iron wire & chains)	essenga
needle	ollodedu pl. illdidi
nest	ngaji ndaridig (the house of the birds)
new	naijuk
night	kawarie
nine	nawdu
nineteen	tomon nawdo
nine times	katitin nawdo
nipples	engurig orrigena
no	menenye
noise	orrori
none	meti, or ētu
no one	mer eldongani (no man)
nose	ngumi pl. ngumeshin
nose bone	ollororom
nostrils	ollgulu ngumi
not	meti, or ētu
nothing	meetoki
now	taāda
number	engeena

O

obey (v. Imp.)	nimining
of (belonging to)	or
often	ngatitin kumuk
oil	ēlara pl. ēelā
old	endasat, morrua (animate objects), msana (inanimate objects)
once	nabu
one	nabu
one hundred	ip
on top	shumata

open (v. Imp.)	tobollo, nebol (Infin.)
orator	ellaigwanan
orchilla weed	narēro
ordure	ingiek
orphan	orgisshi pl. engogishin
ostrich	essidaie pl. sīdan
other	elegai
our	enāang
outside	boo
overflow	etabongori ngare
oversleep	ēemuk
overturn	embēllegenia
owe	nessili (Infin.)
owl	elmagero

P

pain	ēme, or emwi
paint	ossīre
paint (black)	ngugu pl. ngūk
paint (red)	ossoiet lolongoi
paint (white)	endurōto
palaver	orrori
palm	oldiani
pant (v. Imp.)	engebangibang or ebangibang
paper	embalai
papyrus	ollaibolignia, or ollaimütie
partridge	engūrrle pl. engorrlen
pay (v. Imp.)	talagi
penis	enjābu pl. injabok
people	eloshon
perhaps	aāsho
pick (flowers, v. Imp.)	tadoju
pick (up, v. Imp.)	todomu
pig	olbitirr pl. elbitirru
pigeon	endūrrugulu pl. endurruguluni
pigmy	engogi
pig-tail	oldaiiga pl. oldaiigan
pinch (v. Imp.)	etumunu
pipe	olomoti pl. elmotio
point (v. Imp.)	toada

poison	assaiyet, or olniorridue
poison tree	ollmorrije
pools	ngare nairora (lit. the sleeping waters)
poor	oiláīsinan
porcupine	waiaiai pl. iaiya
potato*	ngwashin (kikuyu)
pour (v. Imp.)	tebego {nabeg (sing.)} {negibeg (pl.)} Infin.
place	eweji
plague	oldigana
plain	enguseru pl. engussēro
plantain-eater (green)	engeiwa pl. engeiwan
please (v. Imp.)	enyorr
pleuro-pneumonia	orrgibie
plume (v. Imp.)	irroberringbirr
pray (v. Imp.)	tassai ngai. namon Infin. or ñamon. namor Infin.
precipice	endigirr
pregnant	enduā, or enota ingitok
present	olērinoire
presently	ardi, or tengai
prick (v. Imp.)	kitarrimu
prisoner	atarugagi
property	endogiai
prostitute	eneweje, or dito
pull (v. Imp.)	tierai, niyetu (Infin.)
pull out (v. Imp.)	tebello
punishment	taāra
purgative medicine	oldyanyinyuki, emogotōn, or loodwar
push (v. Imp.)	mbaionia
put (v. Imp.)	eragi {nebi (sing.)} {negiragi (pl.)} Infin.
put off (clothes)	endao engilani
put on (v. Imp.)	enjobo
put out (v. Imp.)	endau, or taara
put out (light)	taā ngima
putrefy (v.)	endungua

---

* The Masai use the kikuyu word, as the potato is only known to them through Wakikuyu medium.

Q

quail	orgēllemi pl. illgēlem
quarrel	etarigeno
quarter	tobelassa
quickly	tassiogi
quiver (for arrows)	emōdien pl. emōdiena

R

rabbit	engīroju pl. engīroju
rain	ngai pl. ngai
rainbow	etau ngolong engang (lit. the boma of the sun)
raise (v. Imp.)	tordomo
rape	essemaiye
rat	nderoni pl. ndēro
raw	erjon
razor	orromōronya pl. ellemororanyi
reach (v. Imp.)	tabaigya
ready	edebi
red	enyuki
refuse (v. Imp.)	erranya nian (Infin.)
remainder	etungai
remember (v. Imp.)	erradamua
repeat (v.)	ngongai taada (Infin.)
resin	enderibenyi
rest	enenenyi
return (v. Imp.)	torrinyoi or inyai $\begin{cases} \text{nairem (sing.)} \\ \text{nerrinyu (pl.)} \end{cases}$ Infin.
rhinoceros	emwoin pl. emwoinyi
rhinoceros-bird	labuak or orlarriaki pl. larriak
rib	ollarassi pl. larass
right hand	ndadeni
rinderpest	ollodua
ring	orrgisoi pl. errgēsso
ringworm	engāmunyän
ripe	eworto
river	ngwasso, or orrgēju, pl. elgegyat
road	ngōītri pl. ngoioitroi

roan antelope	ollbuwa
roof	shumarrotu pl. shumärrotu
root	endāanai pl. endaana
rotten	etomoti, or erradanyi
round	ellgegesat
rub (v. Imp.)	toōju, etüitü
run (v. Imp.)	equet
run away (v. Imp.)	essdoi {nilwaiyer (sing.) / negil waiyer (pl.)} Infin.
rushes	ollgojera

S

safe	esserian
salt	emanyan
sandals	namōka
sand-grouse	enderregogo pl. enderregogo
sap	emānoi
savages	elmangati
say (v. Imp.)	tolimu, or ātoju, Infinitive nēro or negero
scab	orrbolōti pl. illbolōt
scabbard	enjāīshorr pl. enjaishorri
scar	ingiborōī pl. ingiboru
scent	ungwāī
scold (v. Imp.)	endarigyu
secretary-bird	engugogele pl. engugogele
seduce (v. Imp.)	endoraii
see (v.)	nadol (Infinitive)
seeds	enganaiji
sell (v. Imp.)	amer, or teemera
sense	enganyet
set on fire (v. Imp.)	tābejo
seven	nābishana
seventeen	tomon nābishana
seven times	katitin nābishana
sew (v. Imp.)	tereba {naribeshu (sing.) / negerebeshu (pl.)} Infin.
shadow	oloiipi pl. elloiīpi
shake (v. Imp.)	mbiribiru
shake hands	tangassargi
shave (v. Imp.)	tabarrno, or narrbanugi
sheep (a)	ngera

sheep (female)	ngērr pl. ngērra
sheep (female before lambing)	essuben pl. essubeni
sheep (male)	orrmerēgi pl. imerregeshi
shield	elōngo pl. elongoi
shiver (v. Imp.)	engeregera
shoot (v. Imp.)	dangoro, or dara
short	dorop
shoulder	orron pl. irroin, or olloilelai pl. ollailela
show (v. Imp.)	endadua
shrew-mouse	ndedugumi
shut (v. Imp.)	tubuguru $\begin{cases} \text{naigen (sing.)} \\ \text{nigingen (pl.)} \end{cases}$ Infin.
sick (to be)	tollobishi
side	ermatua pl. ematuan
sigh	engeanget, or eanga
sinew	ēngonn, or emorrto
sing (v. Imp.)	ossungoliu $\begin{cases} \text{neeran (sing.)} \\ \text{negerran (pl.)} \end{cases}$ Infin., tarranya
sink (v. Imp.)	mengare
sister	nganashe pl. nganashera
sit (v. Imp.)	tordona $\begin{cases} \text{nardon (sing.)} \\ \text{netornyi (pl.)} \end{cases}$ Infin.
six	elle
sixteen	tomon oiille
six times	kata ille
sixty	ip
skin	oldonyi pl. elonītu
skin (v. Imp.)	iangada
skull	emborroborr pl. mborroborri
sky	shomata
sleep (v. Imp.)	eraga or erora nairora (Infin.)
slip (v. Imp.)	eshērdet
slowly	aketi
small	ngiti
small-pox	endēdiai
smell (v. Imp.)	angwaiye, or engongu
smoke	embūrruer
snail	orrbigitt pl. illbigitu
snake	oloserai pl. ellāsuria
sneeze	engāssini
snipe	ollarrie ngarc
snore (v. Imp.)	erongorong
snow	endūroto

snuff	engisogi
snuff-box	orrgidong pl. irrgidong
sob	essogussu
soft	ernana
soon	eronongorr, or engorr
sore	engerondo pl. engerondoni
sore-eye plant	alangungye
sort	enyaiyu
soup	umōrrorri
spark	eldiēli pl. ediēl
speak (v. Imp.)	atoju, erroro
spear	eremet pl. irrimeti
spear (end)	ollongorat
speech	engigwani
spill (v. Imp.)	mbugoi, or endorai
spine	ollorugot lengurriong
spit (v. Imp.)	tornodoi {nenordargi (sing.) / neginortargi (pl.)} Infin.
spittle	endaishala, or engamolac
splinters	orgeberrati pl. elgeberrat
split (v. Imp.)	tobolossa
spring (of water)	mbagas
spots	elleberbedo, or ildibot
square	errisio
squint	possangu
squirrel	orrgabobo pl. orgedassendari
stamp (v. Imp.)	erroishu
stand (v. Imp.)	itashu {naitashi (sing.) / negendaishi (pl.)} Infin.
star	olāgirra pl. elāgir
stay (v. Imp.)	taanyo, or tordona
steal (v. Imp.)	etuburrōi, negibirro (Infin.)
steinbock	mparnāss
stick	engudi pl. mussidi
sticks (small)	loom pl. elōōm
sticky	eyāda, or ebongishu
still	endegearada
stomach	ngoshogi pl. ngōishoa
stone	ossoiit pl. soiitu
stoop (v. Imp.)	engorroma
strangle (v.)	tagora
striped	geri
stripes	esserat

stroke (v. Imp.)	tooshora
strong	egol
stumble (v. Imp.)	atarŏii
stump	engobē pl. engoben
suck (v. Imp.)	errana, ertanag (Infin.)
suckle (v. Imp.)	endaanga, or endaduagi
sugar-cane	elleropat
sun	ngolong pl. ngolong
sunrise	elebua ngolong
sunset	eradui ngolong
sure	iolo ossubadi (lit. to know well)
surround (v. Imp.)	tamanai
Swahili people	elashomba, enganjura, or lorrida
swallow (v. Imp.)	toiorjoi
swear (v. Imp.)	etamoro, negedek (Infin.)
sweat	engenginyeret
sweep (v. Imp.)	tooro
sweet	emello
swell (v. Imp.)	etejer, or errēia
swim (v. Imp.)	eborrngare
swing (v. Imp.)	iügo
sword	olalim pl. lalima
syphilis*	ngaioulu

T

table	enarra pl. enarrai
tail	orrgidoingai pl. errgidonga
tail-piece (warrior's)	orrgebessi pl. irrgibisseni
take away (v. Imp.)	rodomo or endau (Infin.), naidau
take care of (v. Imp.)	ingorāī
take it	engo
talk (v. Imp.)	toojo
tarantula-spider	engollopa
taste (v. Imp.)	enyorayora
tattoo	orringeriandus
teach (v. Imp.)	keawtageni
tear (v. Imp.)	tobolossa
tears	orrgie pl. errgio
teeth (two front upper)	lalalegishia

* Literally "god knows." The Masai had no knowledge of syphilis until it was introduced amongst them by the Swahilis.

teeth (back)	eldagiligili
tell (v. Imp.)	tiagi, najogi (Infin.)
ten	tomon
ten times	katitin tomon
testicles	ellderege
thank you	aāsi (lit. an expression of delight)
that	lido, or ainyo
their	ejanggarr
there	iddie
these	kolo
they	eninji
thick	sabuk
thief	olaburon, or ossūnguroi pl. essenguru
thigh	engubiss pl. engobessin
thin	rongai
thing	ndoki pl. ndogitin
thirst	engorrei
thirteen	tomonoguni
thirty	ossom
thirty-one	ossomobbo
this	elde, or enā
thorn	orrkigui pl. errēgēgo
thorn tree (black-)	ollongossua
those	leguwa
three	ūni
thrice	katitinuni
throw (v. Imp.)	ondorrai, nananga (Infin.)
thumb	morriukitok, or orrkimojinu sabuk
thunder	egerug ngai
tick	orromashere, or masheri pl. ellemasher
tickle (v. Imp.)	ingitigito
tidy (v. Imp.)	endobera
tight	terresha, or teene
time	ngatitin, or ngatijin
tired	enauari
tobacco	orrgumbau
today	taāda
toe	orrkimojinu pl. irrkimojik
tomato (wild)	endulele
tomorrow	taaiisere
tongs (large)	orramēt
tongs (small, for pulling out hair)	orrbutet

tongue	orrenējap pl. ingejapa
tooth	ollālai pl. lala
tooth-brush	engege
tooth-hole (bottom jaw in centre front where 2 teeth are always extracted)	embwāda
tortoise	olōīguma pl. ollōīguma
touch (v. Imp.)	ūngutuguti
trade	enginyanga
trail (v. Imp.)	engorrtodai
trap	orreshet pl. orresheta
tread upon (v. Imp.)	tāgedo
tree	oldani pl. elgieg
tree (bark used for quivers)	ollokidong
tribe	elōshon pl. olōsho
trumpet	emoworr (lit. horn)
trunk (of tree)	engobē
trunk (of elephant)	engaina (lit. arm)
truth	esseba
try (v. Imp.)	enenanga
turn (v. Imp.)	engorrnaji, embellegenia
turn round (v. Imp.)	belegenia
turtle	olōīguma
twelve	tomon are
twenty	tigitum
twenty-one	tigitum obbo
twice	kātare
twins	ellemāwu
two	ari, or are
two hundred	ip ari

U

udder	orrigena pl. ellgiē
ulcer	olldododai
uncle	engābo
under	ngop, or abori
understand (v. Imp.)	etolingu
unearth (v. Imp.)	tuduru
uphill	ndigin
urine	engolac
use (v. Imp.)	issiashuri

V

vagina	ngumu or engwali
valley	orromoti pl. emotiok
vegetables	mbene
vein	engoň pl. engonya
very	ossūbati
village	engangiti pl. engang
village (warriors)	emanyata pl. emanyat
virgin	engebaigen
voice	egossol, or elduelu
vulture	orlomotonyi pl. elmotonyi
vulture (white)	orrgēleria pl. elgelerrgweni

W

wait (v. Imp.)	ndashu, naanyo (Infin.)
Wakamba	luungŭ
wake (v. Imp.)	enyo
walk (v. Imp.)	alolo, or engurana
wall	essondai pl. ˉessondă
want (v. Imp.)	aiu, naiu (Infinitive)
war	endiore pl. endioria
war-cloth (warrior's)	enanga
warrior	elmorran pl. lamorani
warrior (probationary)	naiseologunia pl. esseologunia (lit. shaven head)
war-song	olloibürri
wart-hog	olbitirr pl. elbitirru
wash (v. Imp.)	aisoja, naijoja (Infin.)
water	ngare
water-buck	olomālu pl. ellemaloni
waterfall	ngare naruga
wealth	olgarrsis
we	eĕog, or iog
well	eloreshu, or orrgēsumet pl. errgesumeti
well (to be)	egolbiero
wet	eshell
what	ainyo, or iya
what for?	ainyo?
what is this?	ainyēna?

what sort?	ainyo?
when	ānu
where	korē
whetstone	engii
which	kore
whiskers (animal's)	elbabit enoret
whisper (v. Imp.)	engōmengōm
whistle (v. Imp.)	essōleshu
white	eborr
who	enaiana
wholly	boōgi
why	ainyo
wild	indim
wild dog	essuyan
wildebeeste	oringat pl. eengati
wind	essiüsiü, or ngijāpi
wind (to make)	ejegāti
window	ellusie pl. ellusiet
wings	naibuku
wipe (v. Imp.)	tudürru
with	alu, or nabo
woman	ngoirraion pl. ngoirroiok, term of opprobrium
	engitok pl. engitua, polite form of address
	essiengegi pl. essiengegin, polite form of address
	endagile, address to young woman
	endamonon, pregnant woman
woman (old)	koko
womb	sabu
wood (used for bellows)	lobōni
work	engias pl. engiaset
workmen	elgunūno
worm	allarrogai pl. lāroga
wound	ingiboirōī pl. ingiboro
wrinkles	engelat ossisin
wrist	errobwada, errobat ngaiina

Y

yam	olaiborriborri
yawn	naiimin
yellow	ngirro
yes	aiye, or anenye

yesterday	ngole
yonder	elleeda, or nyedia
you	iye
your (sing.)	enino
your (plural)	eninyi

Z

zebra	eloidigo pl. eloidigoisho

Printed in the United States
By Bookmasters